# of Contents

ation 6

ction 7

1: How to Decide When to Sell Your Business 9

We Will Learn 9

ght Question 9

ion 14

What to Do In a Fire Sale 15

e Will Learn 15

on 21

The Universe of Potential Buyers 22

e Will Learn 22

ghest Bidder Versus the Right Buyer for Your Business
.... 22

g Beyond the Usual Suspects 24

ching Buyers 27

sion 27

: Putting the Band Together – Assembling Your Deal
.... 28

/e Will Learn 28

nagement Team 28

Advisors 30

ion 47

: How Fast is Fast – Building the Timeline for Your
.... 48

/e Will Learn 48

g for Godot 48

to Help Yourself Manage the Process 52

sion 52

Chapter 6: Getting Our House in Order: Pre-Sale Cl
Organizing Diligence Materials ....

    What We Will Learn ....

    Let's Make Mountains into Molehills ....

    Getting Organized – Preparation for Due Diligence

    Advanced Cleanup ....

    Cleanup, Part Three – Minute Books ....

    Cleanup, Part Four – Intellectual Property ....

    Cleanup, Part Four – Literally Cleaning Up .....

    Conclusion ....

Chapter 7: Running an Auction ....

    What We Will Learn ....

    The Value of An Auction Process ....

    Additional Preparation for the Auction – Reta
    Management ....

    Diligencing the Buyers ....

    Staying Connected ....

        Conclusion ....

Chapter 8: The Letter of Intent ....

    What We Will Learn ....

    Why Letters of Intent are Used ....

    Binding Versus Non-Binding ....

        Confidentiality ....

        Non-Solicitation ....

        Exclusivity ....

    Elements of the LOI ....

    Negotiating Tactics ....

    Conclusion ....

Chapter 9: Deal Structures ....

    What We Will Learn ....

    The Asset Purchase ....

The Stock Purchase 81

The "Stock Swap" or Merger 83

The Exclusive License 86

Conclusion 86

Chapter 10: The Purchase Agreement 88

What We Will Learn 88

The Definitive Agreement 88

Definitions – Why You Care 89

Purchase and Sale Section 91

Closing Mechanics and Termination 99

Seller's Representations and Warranties 100

Buyer's Representations and Warranties 105

Pre-Closing Covenants.. 106

Closing Conditions.. 107

Indemnification 108

"Miscellaneous" Section 111

Signature Pages 112

Exhibits 112

Schedules 113

Conclusion 114

Chapter 11: The Secondary Documents 115

What We Will Learn 115

Employment and Consulting Agreements 115

Transition Services Agreements 118

Bills of Sale, Termination Statements and Assignments 119

Certificates 120

Opinion Letters 121

Flow of Funds 122

Conclusion 122

Chapter 12: What Happens between Signing and Closing 123

What We Will Learn 123

Customers, Vendors and the Landlord 123

Employee Issues: Communications, Meetings and Layoffs . 125

Regulatory Approval, Licenses, Permits 127

Databases and IT Systems 128

Handling Retained Liabilities 128

Conclusion 129

Chapter 13: The Pre-Closing 130

What We Will Learn 130

Preparation 130

Knowing When You are Near the Finish Line 131

The Pre-Closing 134

How to Handle the Bumpy Pre-Closing 135

Conclusion 137

Chapter 14: The Closing 139

What We Will Learn 139

Old School Closings Held In-Person vs. Electronic Closings 139

When is the Closing Finished? 140

What Happens if Something Goes Wrong? 141

Hiding the Ball 143

Conclusion 144

Chapter 15: What Happens After the Closing 145

What We Will Learn 145

The Victory Lap 145

Managing the Transition 146

Getting Paid After the Deal 146

Managing Yourself after the Closing 147

Conclusion 148

Chapter 16: When A Deal Needs to be Called Off 149

What We Will Learn 149

Termination Rights 149

Remedies and Liabilities.. 150

The Morning After – What Happens to the Target Business on a Failed Deal 152

When a Dead Deal Comes Back to Life 153

Conclusion 154

Appendix A – Examples of Tax Impact for Different Sale Structures 155

Acknowledgements... 158

Dedication

To my mother, who has been there through thick and thin.

Introduction

I admire entrepreneurs. It takes a lot of guts to start your own business, rather than work for someone else and get a steady paycheck. Building something out of thin air is a magic trick most civilians don't understand.

When you grow your own business, letting go can be hard. Sometimes it's hard not just emotionally, but financially. I have worked on several dozen mergers and acquisitions, totaling over $6 billion. Some of the transactions were enormous – Thomson's acquisition of Technicolor's global operations. Some were quite small but were life changing for the sellers. Where I practice law in Los Angeles, sometimes my clients will sell their businesses for less than it costs to buy a house here.

In each deal, the hope on both sides – the buyer and the seller – is to get a good deal and have both parties feel like the transaction was a success. Unlike litigation, where everyone wants to fight over every detail, the buying and selling of businesses is usually about taking a seller's business and making it part of something even bigger and better. It's why I really like my work.

This book is going to focus a lot on strategy as well as tactics. Rather than just telling you the mechanics of how to do a deal, I want to share strategies that I have seen work well -- and not so well -- for others. Embarking on a sales process with a clear strategy and goals will make your particular transaction much less of an ordeal.

My goal for the readers of this book is to make the process of selling a business less stressful and more transparent. If this book can help a business owner get the best value for the owner's pride and joy and manage their sales process in a way that's smooth and reasonably fair, I'll be a happy author.

Lastly, as any good lawyer would do, I obviously need to let you know that this book is not intended to serve as legal advice. Everybody's situation is different, and you would be wise to take the things you learn in this book and consult with your own lawyer, if only to make sure the law hasn't changed since the most recent publication date of this book.

Chapter 1: How to Decide When to Sell Your Business

What We Will Learn

This chapter is designed to stimulate you to pre-plan for a successful exit. We will look at other people's life lessons to think about timing our sale.

The Right Question

Many entrepreneurs start thinking about how to sell their businesses by thinking about how much the sales price will be.

I suggest that the better starting point is to ask "why now?" rather than "how much?"

We are going to look at selling our business from two very different perspectives. First, we will approach a potential sale from the perspective of those of you that are just starting to think about selling your business. In the next chapter, we will think about how to handle a sale for those who need to sell their businesses yesterday.

Building an Exit Strategy

Working through our question – "why now?" – will help us figure out our goals for our deal. Whether you have made the actual decision to sell, or are just starting to ponder whether and when to sell, we should try to establish a framework for making the decision intelligently. This section is intended to reveal potential blind spots as you start your process.

Retirement planning

If you are ten years away from retirement, you are probably in an ideal spot to start planning for a successful exit.

As you build your exit strategy, ask yourself:

- How much of my net worth is tied up in the business?

  - Would I _like_ to keep working part time at the business if I can afford to completely walk away?

  - Do I _need_ to keep working part time if I can't afford to completely walk away?

- Do I have family that are employees or otherwise drawing income from the business?

- How much of my lifestyle is supported by the business?

  - Do I lease my car through the business?

  - Do I use business conventions or educational conferences to cover vacation travel?

  - Do I run other expenses through the business like season tickets for baseball or charitable activities that I like to sponsor?

- Will the sales proceeds generate enough of an income stream that will cover my expenses in retirement?

Health and Age

If you are experiencing health issues or are just slowing down a bit as the aging process works its inevitable magic, you should think about these additional factors:

- If you have serious health problems, you will want to look into the cost of replacement health insurance now, rather than after a deal. On a related note, if you may be eligible for Medicare, checking to see if your particular health needs will be covered under Medicare is worth doing now.

  - If you can't get coverage or can't afford the coverage that is available, you may want to craft your business sale to include keeping you on in some capacity to address your health issues.

- If your age is the driver, the sooner you sell the better. Most healthy businesses are driven by relationships with customers and vendors. A buyer will need to "acquire" your relationships as well as the employees and physical assets. The buyer will likely need your assistance in doing a hand-off, so doing it while you have the energy will likely serve you better than worrying about maximizing a sale to get every last dollar.

- If you don't view your age as an issue, but your spouse or kids do, you might consider crafting an exit where you locate a successor to buy out your business over time, which could allow you to continue working but at a reduced pace. This kind of strategy would help you avoid quitting cold turkey.

Industry Sea Change

If concerns about where your industry is headed are causing you to think about a sale, more often than not your instincts are probably right. In the era of Uber, I personally wouldn't want to own a taxi business.

The key factors for you to consider when building your exit strategy here would be:

How Long Until the Business Becomes Obsolete?

Making a judgment call on how long your part of the industry will be able to keep chugging along. Is the industry going to fall off a cliff tomorrow, or limp along for a few (or several) years?

I was part of the legal team that helped a large French company, Thomson, buy Technicolor in 2001. Being brilliant large firm lawyers, we looked at each other and thought our client was goofy to buy Technicolor. In the dot com era, we looked at Technicolor as a technological dinosaur – surely film was going away and we'd all be watching movies on the internet and not on stupid DVDs. However, in 2005, Technicolor was still selling billions of dollars of DVDs and was moving into digital cinema. I sheepishly asked for a job there after the software company I was working at as general counsel imploded. In 2016, people are still buying DVDs. Dinosaur, you say.

Can the Business Evolve?

Can your part of the industry or product offering be repurposed toward another viable but less profitable opportunity so it's still sellable?

Your Particular Product Offering is Long in the Tooth

If we are contemplating selling because your industry is healthy but you haven't invested in refreshing your product line or kept up with technological changes, you will need to plan to address these factors:

- Would you be better off tweaking the product to make the product more current before you start a sales process?

- Would a competitor still see value in acquiring the older offering you have because it is still better than what they have to offer?

- Do we have multiple products and have an opportunity to sell products that are still desirable while dropping or de-emphasizing the outdated offerings?

You Received an Unsolicited Offer

Perhaps you purchased this book because you have actually received an offer, or at least an invitation to start a conversation about selling, and need to figure out what to do.

At a minimum, you should be flattered. Someone thinks your business is a valuable property!

The key in this situation is to be measured in your approach. You don't want to let the flattery or excitement cause you to rush you toward a less than optimal result. You will want to think through before you invest significant time and money on hiring advisors:

- Is the business just starting to take off? If you sell now, do you leave value on the table?

- Many times a buyer will want the management to stay involved, at least for a decent stretch of time, sometimes for six to twelve months. How do you feel about having a boss? What if you get overruled on decisions you used to make on your own?

- How do you know what a fair price is? Do you have competitors who have sold and know what they received?

- Does the business have skeletons in the closet that need to be dealt with before you sell?

- Does the business support a lifestyle that you may not be able to maintain on an employee's salary?

- What kind of reputation does the prospective buyer have? Is the buyer a tire kicker, hoping to get a free look at its competitor – you? Does the buyer have the funds to do a deal? Do they renege on deals?

Conclusion

By working through this chapter, you have started thinking strategically about selling your business. Next, we are going to look at what to do if a business is in dire straits and has to conduct a "fire sale".

Chapter 2: What to Do In a Fire Sale

What We Will Learn

I this chapter, we talk about what to do if you bought this book because you have to sell the business right away or have actually signed a letter of intent. Remember, every crisis is just an opportunity in disguise.

Selling a Business That's Out of Money

It happens. A business loses a major customer with no foreseeable replacement customer on the horizon. Management places a bet on expanding and gets overextended.

Colin Powell, the former US Chief of Staff for the military, likes to say sometimes problems look less scary the next morning. If you have looked at the same problem every morning for a month, it's probably time to make a change. Sometimes that means doubling down, sometimes that means cutting your losses.

If you are selling because you can't afford to stay in business, then you need to work through an emergency checklist rather than hope to get lucky and sell our business in 48 hours or less. You need to focus first on giving yourself enough runway to sell rather than simply focusing directly on selling.

What advice can help in this kind of situation?

Your Responsibilities May Have Changed

Entrepreneurs sometimes get confused about who has the final say on an acquisition.

If your company is healthy, the board, and ultimately the owners of your company's equity, get the final say in whether to sell the business and for how much.

If your company's balance sheet is upside down – the company's liabilities are greater than its assets – or worse, the odds are good that you are about to miss a payroll – then the board and the management team have to answer to a different set of masters. The board and management team need to consider what is best for the company's creditors ahead of what's best for the shareholders.

Before you proceed with a sale in this kind of situation, you would be well advised to engage a lawyer and go through a quick analysis of your fiduciary duties to your company's different constituencies.

Extend the Runway

In a "going out of business" scenario, our first mission is to extend our ability to survive until you can close a sale of the business.

Unless you have a competitor who has been hounding you to sell, the odds are good that (like most sellers), it will take a few months to find the right buyer at a remotely fair price, and a few additional months to close the sale. We will walk through a timeline to get to a closing in the next chapter, but right now, you need to assume it's not going to be a quick process.

If you only have thirty seconds on the shot clock, you need to reset the clock.

Here's how you do it.

Burn Rate

In the tech startup world, my clients talk a lot about their "burn rate." They look at how much their operations cost each month, soup to nuts – that's the company's "burn rate." Then they divide the amount of actual cash in the bank by the monthly burn. We're not counting accounts receivable, no matter how much "certainty" we have on collectability. If we have $500K in cash and our operating cost is $200K, then our runway is 2 ½ months, assuming no new cash comes in the door.

The 2 ½ month number is how fast our company could go under. If customers pay and pay on time, maybe we live a little longer. However, we assume everything goes wrong and customers short pay (a customer owes $100 but pays $50 this month) and slow pay (a customer is obligated to pay on 30 days from invoice, but pays 90 days out).

Whatever we can legally do to raise the number of months we can operate, we're going to do it.

Immediate Layoff.

If we are selling because we lost a major customer, we are going to do a layoff. Period.

Anyone who does not directly contribute to making or selling products has to go.

You no longer need a receptionist. Get a phone system that offers a directory.

Consultants need to be terminated. Public relations, marketing, "strategic advice" – they all need to go, immediately.

Sales should not be immune. A sales person that costs more than he brings in has to go. Now.

If you have engineers working on new products that you are not currently selling, and can't sell in the next few months, then the engineers have to go have to go. Sometimes engineering types like to solve "problems" that fascinate them but don't actually solve a problem that a customer is willing to pay to solve. That has to stop immediately.

Layoffs cost money. They are scary to the remaining employees, to your customers, to your vendors and probably to you too. However, if revenues minus costs equal a negative number, and have for some time, you will need to "right size" your business to make it more attractive.

But wait – if we do a layoff and then try to sell our business, won't buyers think the business is sinking and low ball us?

Probably, but here's the alternative:

- We don't do a layoff.

- The losses continue.

- If we only have 2-3 months of cash left before the business has to close, the business may end up closing before we can even start talking to buyers. It normally takes weeks to find a buyer, and then a few months to close a deal.

    o If a buyer magically appears and makes us an offer in a week, they will ask to see your financial statements. When they see the financial statements, they will see that you only have a few months of cash and are sinking. You will end up with a low-ball price anyway.

    o Worse – the buyer sees your financials, and decides to wait until your business closes. Then they get your customers and employees for free and your hard assets for pennies in a liquidation sale. Yikes.

Said simply, without immediate cost cutting, the Vegas odds of having to close the doors and get nothing for the business go waaaay up.

Pay Cuts

The twin sister of a layoff is the pay cut.

Layoff survivors get pay cuts or get added to the list of terminated employees. Owners have to be at the front of the line to take a pay cut. It's part of the joy of being a leader.

Slow Pay Vendors

If our burn rate is too high, you may need to contemplate slowing down your payment of invoices. If you are paying non-critical vendors within 30 days of their invoices, you may need to consider going to 45 or 60 days.

Notice we said "non-critical" vendors. Vendors will notice immediately when you start to slow pay. Vendors who are critical – you sell remanufactured ink cartridges and have only one source of fresh ink – probably should be treated gingerly. But non-critical functions – copy machine, coffee for the breakroom, etc. probably deserve a look.

That being said, slow paying employees is a recipe for a lawsuit or regulatory fines, especially in a state like California. It's rarely worth doing.

Ask Vendors for Discounts

This category is just free money. It's not fun calling a vendor to demand a "loyalty" discount, a volume discount or a discount just because I want a discount, but all it costs you is a phone call and some short term stress for the vendor. Just don't get overly muscular with vendors that you need or may run into again in your next business.

Pull Forward Customer Payments

If your business is in trouble in February, and you have customer payments due in October, it may be time to ask customers to pay in March in return for a significant percentage discount. You will have to weigh the risk of scaring customers against the benefit of cash in the bank. That being said, everyone loves a discount, especially if it's on something like an annual software license where no physical products are being delivered every month.

If you work this kind of process, you can go from flying the plane into the side of the mountain to a crash landing in the trees. The key is to be able to walk away from the plane, and working your process will get you to that place.

Conclusion

If you are in a rough spot, you now have some ideas on how to get enough runway to reach a reasonably successful sales result. Next, we will look at the time it will take to make our exit and how to manage deal costs.

Chapter 3: The Universe of Potential Buyers

What We Will Learn

One might think sorting out the best buyer for your business is pretty easy. The best buyer is the buyer who offers the highest price.

Well, maybe. If a buyer offers you $10 million and only pays you $1 million a year for ten years, you might find yourself having to sue the buyer to get the last nine payments. If you are told you can stay on as an employee as long as you like, and you get fired two months after selling your business, that could be disastrous. While your lawyer can help you negotiate and guide you on what terms are "market", you are the ultimate decision maker and will have to bear the brunt of the risks you are willing to take.

This chapter is focused on finding the right buyer for your business. We want to do a 360-degree look at every category of buyer and make sure we don't leave any stones unturned as we try to get the right result for your company's constituencies. This chapter will illuminate the buyer categories we should review before starting our process.

The Highest Bidder Versus the Right Buyer for Your Business

In Chapter 1, we thought about the motivations behind your purchase of this book. Now, let's apply those different scenarios to selecting a buyer.

Buyers to Cash Us Out

If the goal is to create a cash pile for retirement or get out of a situation where we can't run the business much longer due to age or health concerns, then your thought process will be geared toward purely financial outcomes.

In this case, we want a buyer that will score well on the following factors:

- Pay the highest total purchase price
- Pay the biggest piece of the purchase price up front
- Pay in cash and not stock (or at least in publicly tradable stock not private company stock)
- Have little room to claw back the purchase price
- Requires little to no additional time from you after the deal closes
- If your company gets broken into pieces by the new buyer and sold off for its parts, or a layoff happens right before or after the sale, you won't agonize over it for the next several years

Buyers to Keep You Employed

If the business can't be sold for a sum that is large enough to permit you to comfortably retire, then you may also want a buyer who is committed to hire us for an extended period of time.

Similarly, if the company's team is composed of rock star software engineers but the company's products aren't successful, you may be able to find a buyer who doesn't want the business, but really wants the engineering team. This kind of deal is referred to in the tech world as an "acqui-hire".

This might seem a little counterintuitive, but if the reason we are considering a sale is because the business has stale products and can't afford to create new offerings through research and development, then finding a buyer who can invest funds to grow the business back to health while allowing you to retain a partial ownership may help you unlock more wealth for yourself than if you continue on your own without the extra rocket fuel. Similarly, if your business has two out of three products that your customers need, but building that third product on your own is out of reach, joining forces with a company that has the third product may be better for all parties.

Looking Beyond the Usual Suspects

Having determined the kind of buyer that you are likely to want, let's now look at the universe of potential buyers through the lens you have picked for yourself.

Competitors

If you want to go with the highest bidder, you should consider our competitors.

The upside of considering competitors is they will consist of a lot of obvious candidates. Competitors will understand the value that your company's products, services, employees and brand bring to the table much more quickly than other potential buyers who need to learn about your company and your industry.

The downside is that once you start contacting them, even with a confidentiality agreement in place, the odds are higher than not that word will get out into the street, impacting our relationships with customers, vendors and employees.

Strategic Buyers

Investment bankers and deal lawyers consider competitors to be strategic buyers. However, strategic buyers also include vendors, customers and "near-competitors."

Depending on your business, the businesses that sell products to you may see that your profit margins are better than theirs. They may see that they can sell more of their products if they own your business. Sometimes, they will have the thought that they could run your business better than you – and for the right price you may welcome them to take on that challenge.

Customers may take a similar view, looking at a purchase of your business as a way to lower their costs and improve their own margins by having your company under their umbrella.

A "near-competitor" is a company that may not directly compete with you but operates next to you in the same customer base. If your company sells mining safety devices and my company sells mining equipment on a larger scale, I may see your company as a nice "tuck-in" with my existing product lines.

The upside with the other strategic buyers are similar to the competitor category. The buyers in this category already know your business or can get up to speed on your business quickly because they understand your industry. They can also start imagining the benefits of an acquisition for themselves, possibly considering additional benefits (or "synergies" in acquisition-speak) that may not have crossed your mind.

The downside is also similar. Word could get out fairly quickly once you approach this category.

Financial Buyers – Private Equity

Large investment firms may see the benefit to owning your business. Private equity funds are businesses that look for companies that have flaws that the funds believe they can fix. The fund may think that a target company has a tired management team, outdated product offerings, a lack of capital investment, is undercapitalized or aiming at the wrong customer base.

If the fund acquires the business, its likely goal is to clean it up and then sell the business again five years later.

The odds are also good that the fund will look at the roster of employees and do a layoff shortly after the deal closes. The fund may also have its own ideas on who it would like to manage the company. Many times, the fund will have seasoned veterans from other companies that it ran and sold, and will call on them to come in to turn the business around. If you are looking for a company to retain you for a long period, you should tread carefully with financial buyers.

Employees

Sometimes the most obvious buyer is actually sitting outside your office door. Or if you are not a shareholder, but part of the company's management, the buyer could be sitting in your chair.

If management or key employees think that they can run the business, they might be willing to find a financing source (the bank, a private equity fund, a strategic lender) and make a run at buying the business. If the goal is to retire, the owners may want to consider offering the business to the existing team.

The upside is the equity holders already know the buyers and the timeline to a sale may be relatively short.

The downside includes the risk that the owner may get seller's remorse after the deal and not want to go away completely. There is also a risk that the buyers may not be able to offer the best price and then quit if the owner tries to find alternative buyers. Lastly, the owner may wonder why the buyers didn't do things better while they were employees.

Approaching Buyers

If your business is small and the number of buyers is limited, you may attempt to find a buyer on your own or use a business broker, discussed in the next chapter.

Most larger, sophisticated businesses should at least consider hiring an investment banker to conduct some form of auction for them.

The risks of conducting an auction include alerting competitors, customers, vendors and possibly employees that your business is for sale. If you are unable to complete a sale transaction, you may have to wait a while before trying to sell your business, since prospective buyers will wonder if your business didn't sell because it had too many issues.

While these are risks to consider, using an investment banker to think creatively about the range and number of buyers who might be interested in your business usually generates higher prices.

Conclusion

In this chapter you have considered who the right buyer is for your particular set of goals. You looked at a wide range of buyer categories to determine what types of buyers you want to approach. You are now ready to start putting the team together.

Chapter 4: Putting the Band Together – Assembling Your Deal Team

What We Will Learn

In this chapter we are going to look at how to put together the deal team you will need to manage the sales process. We will review the role of each team member. We will also focus on what the engagement letter for an investment banker contains.

The Management Team

The trickiest part of assembling your team will be figuring out which employees need to know that you intend to sell the business.

Ultimate Decision Maker Versus Management Point Person

For small businesses, the owner/CEO will be the ultimate decision maker and the gatekeeper for the sale transaction.

For larger companies, the deal may be better served by having someone other than the owner/CEO handling day to day negotiations to allow the CEO to be kept in reserve to talk principal-to-principal when major points need to be resolved. If the CEO is kept out of the main fray, the selling company will need to have a point person to coordinate the team. Usually, the point person will be the selling company's chief financial officer or head of business development. The keys to selecting a good point person are: (a) solid understanding of the business, (b) the ability to make critical employees respond quickly when they are needed for the deal and (c) the ability to quickly get the CEO's attention when needed.

For most companies with twenty employees or more, the CEO will bring the chief financial officer, the head of sales and the person in charge of building the company's products or services (plant manager, chief technology officer, etc.).

Other Employees

Generally speaking, the smaller the circle of employees who know about the deal, the better.

Why?

In virtually every company, the employees represent a key asset of the company. If you inform your employees that the company is for sale before a sale actually happens, you run a serious risk that the employees capable of leaving for other jobs will do just that, as they look for job security in what they perceive as a more stable company. If you can keep the sales process from frightening the employee base until you are close to finishing a sale, then your odds of retaining the key employees for the buyer improve, as you will now be in a position to explain to employees who the buyer is and what the buyer's intentions are for the employees.

Obviously, the longer a transaction takes, and the more strange people wearing Armani suits in the office lobby keep appearing, the word may get out in spite of your best efforts. However, letting the word out early does nothing to further your own interests and could cause truly unnecessary stress for employees who may end up as part of an even bigger, more stable employment situation.

As time goes on and you have a letter of intent with a buyer, you can broaden the circle to include key parts of the finance, manufacturing, sales and research & development teams, since the buyer will want to interview them at points during their review of the business. Near the mid-point of a deal, it's also good to bring the human resources team into the loop, so they can interact with the buyer's HR team on coordinating benefits and things like transitioning employees from one payroll system to another.

The key is to involve the right employees at the right time on a "need to know" basis.

Outside Advisors

Depending on the size and complexity of your business, you may need a number of advisors to help you. At a minimum, you will need to involve an accountant to advise you on the tax implications of your deal structure and a lawyer to negotiate the deal terms and document the transaction. You may also hire an investment banker or business broker. We will go through each of these categories individually, to start the process of thinking who you need, for what, and when.

The Accountant

What You Need:

At a minimum, you will need to produce accurate financial statements and a general ledger to satisfy most buyers.

The financial statements that a buyer wants to see are:

- Your income statement to see profits and losses.
- Your balance sheet, to see assets and liabilities.
- Your cash flow statement, to see how healthy the company is now and is expected to be in the near future.

If you are a small business owner running an ice cream shop, you may be using Quickbooks. If you are comfortable, you may be able to produce this information on your own. If you are not comfortable, or "sort of" comfortable, you will be much better off investing in having an actual certified public accountant, or CPA, look at your books.

A good CPA can confirm that you have been entering revenue and expenses correctly, and putting assets and liabilities into the correct categories.

If you are running a business that generates significant sums, you probably already have a CPA. However, the CPA will need to understand that your needs are now changing from maximizing deductions on your tax return to maximizing deal value in a potential sale.

When you have a CPA, the buyer may ask for one of three different categories of review of the company's financial statements by your CPA. The lowest level of review is financial statements that are unaudited and unreviewed – these are the financial statements that you printed out using Quickbooks with no input from the CPA. The second level is a set of financial statements that have been reviewed but are unaudited, meaning the CPA checked your math, but is not offering an opinion on how accurate the company's categorization of different expenses and income items are. The highest level is a set of audited financials, where the CPA actually gives an opinion confirming that the CPA not only checked the math but also checked to make sure that the company's financial statements actually applied the correct rules on how data was to be categorized and interpreted, usually with the standard being that the financial statements complied with generally accepted accounting principles, or "GAAP".

The accountant will be important for helping with other matters as well.

You will want a good tax advisor to help you. You will want the accountant to be able to review deal structures with you. As we will discuss later, there can be very large differences on how much tax you pay when you sell your business, depending on whether you sell your company's assets or you personally sell the stock of the company to a buyer. On the same note, if your company sells its assets, how the purchase price is allocated across the assets could have a big impact on the selling company and the buyer. If your regular accountant has limited experience with mergers and acquisitions, you may want to involve a tax lawyer, especially if a lot of money is on the line for you.

The accountant will also be able to help you respond to the buyer's requests for financial information. If your company has a chief financial officer, that person can do the lion's share of responding to requests for a list of accounts payable or the rental payment history for your buildings for the last five years. If you don't have a chief financial officer, or your chief financial officer does not have the time to do her normal job and respond to questions, the accountant can serve as a liaison. Alternatively, if you do not have a chief financial officer, you may want to hire an interim chief financial officer to get you through the deal.

Lastly, more sophisticated buyers will perform a quality of earnings analysis on your business. In simple terms, the buyer's accounting team will look at the business's financial statements and back out owner compensation and unusual expenses (Dodger season tickets, BMW leases, country club memberships, cell phone bills, etc.). This is called "normalizing" the earnings. A smart seller will understand that a quality of earnings report is frequently used by a buyer to negotiate the purchase price. You will want to have an accountant on your side to be able to argue against purchase price adjustments based on items coming out of the quality of earnings report.

Who Do You Pick?

If you are a small business owner, the CPA who does your taxes every year may be just fine.

If you have a larger business, you probably want an accounting firm that has experience in your industry and with mergers and acquisitions. While a solo CPA who does individual tax planning may be able to file basic corporate tax returns, for a life changing event like the sale of your business, you may want to hire a firm with specific business sale experience.

You will also want to have your "deal" accountant be available during all kinds of weather. If you expect to close your sale transaction in March or April, it would be unfortunate if your regular CPA is unavailable at critical moments because of individual tax season.

When Do I Hire the Accountant?

The accountant is a key part of the deal team. You need to bring on the accountant / tax lawyer as soon as you are truly committed to selling the business.

If we wait until after we sign a letter of intent with a buyer, it will be too late. We will explain what happens at the letter of intent stage shortly, but the letter of intent sets out the deal structure. If you attempt to negotiate the letter of intent without an accountant or lawyer, you may very well agree to an asset sale that is painful from a tax perspective, when the accountant or lawyer may have been able to figure out a different, more tax-efficient structure for you.

What's This Going to Cost Me?

Understanding that the accountant's business client will be going away, the accountant will most likely want to be paid on an hourly basis. The key for the business owner is to get the accountant's services and fees in writing.

The accounting relationship is usually covered in an engagement letter. The accountant's engagement letter should lay out:

- What services will be provided (just looking at Quickbooks? Filing late returns? Responding to diligence requests? Strategic or valuation advice? Preparing or revising financial statements?)

- Who will actually be performing the work (the person you met? Her junior accountants? People in other offices?)

- The hourly rate for each person that will work on your deal.

- The retainer – an upfront deposit that the accountant can apply to one of their bills if you are late or miss paying them.

The owner should request an estimate, understanding it's an estimate and not a hard promise.

The Lawyer

What You Need

Your "deal" lawyer will be your guide through the process, especially if you do not have an investment banker.

The lawyer should review all contracts between you and the buyer. If you involve the lawyer in the negotiations for the letter of intent, it will spare you from having to "unscramble the egg" and renegotiate deal points in the letter that a first time seller may not have understood. The lawyer will help you think through the right structure.

In a typical sale with only one buyer, the buyer's lawyer will draft the purchase agreement. The seller's lawyer will review the purchase agreement and all additional agreements and give you guidance on what to negotiate.

The seller's lawyer will also help you put together and negotiate the disclosure schedule. The disclosure schedule gets covered in greater detail later, but for now understand that the schedules provide additional information to the buyer required by the purchase agreement itself.

The lawyer, if you need one, can also help you organize and present information that the buyer requests from the business. A smart buyer will want copies of customer and vendor contracts, any leases, documents covering intellectual property, and information about litigation if you have any. A good lawyer can help you sort through what you need to disclose and what is trivial. For sensitive matters, the lawyer can also give you strategic guidance on how to explain difficult stories about the business in a way that's honest without doing a chicken little routine and causing you to be fearful where it's not justified.

It's just a fact of life that larger deals frequently require additional specialist lawyers.

If you have a heavily regulated business like a medical practice or insurance firm, the lead lawyer may recommend hiring (or using your existing) regulatory lawyer to make sure that necessary licenses are able to be transferred and that the seller and buyer get any required agency or governmental approvals.

If the business owns significant real estate properties, using a real estate lawyer for that piece of the deal may be wise. If the business's facilities have any environmental issues, the seller may want to engage environmental counsel or environmental assessment experts to quantify any liability issues with spills or leaks.

Lastly, if the sale is going to generate a serious payday for the owners, the owners may want to think about bringing in an estate planning lawyer toward the end of the transaction to figure out the most tax-efficient way to manage the payout when it comes.

For smaller deals like the sale of a yoga studio for $100,000 using a business broker, the business broker will usually provide some guidance on when you may need to engage an attorney.

Who Do You Pick?

Lawyers come in a variety of flavors. For the sale of your business, you want a lawyer experienced in selling businesses. This is not the time to use your estate planning lawyer or your litigation guy.

While it's optimal to hire a deal lawyer who is intimately familiar with your industry, the key is whether the lawyer has worked on a variety of deal structures (asset sale, stock sale, mergers) and has worked for both buyers and sellers. If you are selling a medical spa business and insist on only using a deal lawyer who has worked on medical spa sale transactions, you may have to look under quite a few rocks to find one.

You will be working very closely with the lawyer you select, so you will want to make sure you have a good personality fit. Any deal will bring time pressures, contentious deal points and difficult judgment calls. Having a lawyer that you trust and knowing that the lawyer understands what's normal and what's not will serve you well.

When Do You Hire The Lawyer?

Much like the accountant, hiring the lawyer before you negotiate a letter of intent is critical. If you hand the lawyer a signed letter of intent, even if it's not binding, the lawyer's ability to dig you out of a point that you didn't understand or didn't appreciate will be pretty limited.

Optimally, you will hire the lawyer before engaging with an investment banker so the lawyer can guide you through the contract with them.

What's This Going to Cost Me?

Much like the "sell side" accountant, the lawyer will likely want to be paid hourly. Experienced lawyers should be able to look at the likely size of the sale, the complexity of the deal structure and the amount of time needed and arrive at a decent estimate before accepting the engagement.

Like the accountant, the lawyer should offer an engagement letter, laying out:

- What services will be provided (review of the deal documents? Assistance with diligence? Handling the entire sales transaction? Excluding tax advice?)

- Who will actually be performing the work (The person you met? A different partner? Junior lawyers? People in other offices?)

- The hourly rate for each person who will work on your deal.

- The retainer – an upfront deposit that the lawyer use to cover late bills.

Business Brokers

What You Need

For smaller businesses (think a restaurant franchise), a seller may want to market the sale of the business using a business broker.

A business broker functions a lot like a real estate agent, and in states like California, are registered with the state real estate department.

The broker can help you figure out the initial value of your business if you are struggling with determining a price that the market will accept. The broker may help you draft a very simple description of your business to be distributed to potential buyers, called a confidential information memorandum.

The broker may do an initial screening of buyers. They will look to sort out serious buyers from potential "tire kickers". They may also check out each buyer's ability to finance the purchase.

The business broker will likely list your business on their website and possibly a larger website like BizBen or BizBuySell. These services are very similar to the multiple listing service, or MLS, that real estate agents use to sell homes.

If buyers surface, the business broker will help you answer questions about your business and assist with negotiating the purchase price.

Who Do You Pick?

If you use a business broker, you will want a person dedicated to selling businesses. Sometimes, a real estate agent will do business brokerage work on the side and may not be able to provide more than rudimentary assistance. Believe it or not, I have met business brokers who were wearing track suits.

Like real estate agents, the business broker may want to represent both the buyer and the seller in the transaction, taking the position that the broker represents the "deal", not the individual parties. This isn't always a bad thing if you meet a well-connected business broker. However, the obvious concern here is the business broker could easily up being motivated to sell the business to get the broker's commission as quick as possible, not to get the best transaction for the seller. As an example, if you receive (a) an offer for $1,000,000 in cash today from one buyer versus (b) a second offer for $500,000 today and $600,000 a year from now, the broker may be motivated to push the second offer to get the higher commission, even though you as the seller may be at risk if the second seller can't come up with the cash a year from now or wants to argue about whether the business you sold had hidden flaws that you did not disclose.

Business brokers usually recommend that sellers structure their deals as asset sales. Normally, a seller prefers to sell the stock of her company to get a lower tax rate on the sale. The business broker has an issue specific to the broker though – under the securities laws, business brokers can't be involved in a steady stream of stock sales. They can usually participate in the sale of a business's assets.

The broker will also offer the use of a form of asset purchase agreement. Again, using a simple template that balances each party's interests will save money on lawyers. However, if your business is worth a substantial amount in your view, you may end up giving up substantial points to save a few thousand dollars.

The business broker will also want an escrow agent to participate in the transaction. When it comes time to close the business sale, the buyer will send the purchase price to the escrow agent. When the assets pass to the buyer, the escrow agent will send over the purchase price to the seller . . . minus the broker's commission. There may be good reasons to put the money in escrow to protect each side (filing a bulk sales notice when the business has inventory, dealing with employment-related regulatory issues), but the escrow mechanism guarantees the broker will get paid. The broker worries that the seller, who is obligated to pay the broker (not the buyer), will decide after the fact that the broker didn't do enough to earn the fee.

When Do You Hire the Business Broker?

If your business is small, you can hire the business broker shortly after you hire the accountant.

What's This Going to Cost Me?

Like other consultants, brokers may charge hourly fees, retainers or success fees. Most business brokers I have met will ask for a non-refundable retainer up front and then charge a success fee or commission equal to 10% of the total purchase price.

The broker will provide a listing agreement, similar to listing a house. The agreement will list the specific services being provided and explain how they are compensated.

The definition of "consideration" is important. "Consideration" means what gets counted when determining the final sales price for purposes of figuring out the broker's commission.

If the sale price is just $1,000,000 paid in cash at the closing, the consideration is just $1,000,000.

If the sale price is $500,000 paid at the closing, $500,000 paid a year later and the assumption of the seller's bank loans for $300,000, the definition of consideration gets a lot more interesting. The broker may use a definition that counts the $500,000 to be paid a year later as actually counting now and ask for their 10% slice today instead of waiting a year, at risk to the broker. Similarly, although the seller isn't receiving any cash when the buyer assumes the $300,000 loan, the broker would like a fee equal to 10% of the loan since the broker delivered the economic benefit to the seller of getting rid of the economic burden of having to repay the loan.

Reading the consideration definition closely is a key part of signing the listing agreement.

The listing agreement may also have a "tail" provision. If the broker introduces you to a potential buyer and then you terminate the listing agreement, the broker would still like to get paid if you close a deal with the buyer later. We will discuss the "tail" in greater detail in the next section on investment bankers.

Investment Bankers

What You Need

If you are selling a business that is generating $2,000,000 or more in revenue, you probably will want to use an investment banker.

Investment bankers are very different from the commercial banker that helps with deposits and loans.

A true investment banker is registered with FINRA, the Financial Industry Regulatory Authority. While FINRA is not a government agency, it is the organization that registers and supervises the activities of investment professionals involved in the offer and sale of securities. A registered investment banker can help you sell your company's assets or the stock of your company without tripping over the securities laws. Some folks will call themselves investment bankers but are not registered with FINRA – their ability to help on a sale transaction is limited, much like the business brokers.

The investment banker can offer a wide range of services.

While an investment banker can offer guidance about the initial value of your business, the investment banker, or investment banker for short, will do much more than help set a sales price. The investment banker will give you guidance on making the business more attractive for sale and get you ready for the ultimate buyer's due diligence investigations. Rather than going with the first legitimate offer, the investment banker will try to get a bidding war going. The bidding war is usually referred to as an auction. A good auction has a number of steps to it – getting indications of interest, initial diligence followed by a letter of intent, and a final round of negotiating letters of intent with truly interested potential buyers.

Normally, the investment banker will work with you to create a "story" about the business – why the business, its assets, its technology, its people, its customer base are incredibly valuable. The investment banker will create marketing materials to support the story and promote it – an initial "teaser" document, a full confidential information memorandum and answers to follow up questions from interested prospects. The investment banker's materials will usually go much farther in depth than the materials that a business broker would prepare.

The investment banker will actively canvas the market for potential buyers, rather than just listing your business on a website. The investment banker will think creatively about the universe of potential buyers, considering not just competitors, but customers, vendors and possible financial buyers such as private equity firms that primarily buy existing businesses, grow them and then re-sell them. The investment banker will manage the sales process and communications with buyers so the owners can run the business.

Ideally, the investment banker should be able to analyze potential offers and provide advice on pros and cons of each offer as they roll in. The investment banker will focus on more than just economics, pointing out where treatment of liabilities, handling of employees, timing of payments, credit risk with a particular buyer and other matters come into play in grading a given offer.

Much like a lawyer, the investment banker can also serve as the "bad cop" to the management team's good cop if negotiations bog down or become contentious. Investment bankers tend to be pretty sturdy folks and are hard to ruffle.

The investment banker also brings a different level of sophistication to the negotiations. While the management may be excellent at negotiating with customers, the investment banker will know what's market for acquisitions and can give valuable insights into when a first time seller is being taken for a ride.

Who Do You Pick?

A registered FINRA investment bank is our first and last pick.

If the investment banker has a consistent stream of deals in your size range and industry, he will bring great value to your deal. If your deal is a little too small compared to the other investment banker's clients, you will want assurances that your deal will still get the investment banker's personal attention and not land on a more junior investment banker's desk.

Unlike business brokers, investment bankers do not represent both sides in a deal, so you will have their loyalty. That being said, investment bankers that do "buy side" and "sell side" deals may occasionally have a seller that is a perfect fit with a buyer that the investment bank has represented before. Having a healthy conversation about conflicts of interest is always a good thing to cover early.

When do You Hire the Investment Banker?

We should hire the investment banker after we hire the accountant and the lawyer. Optimally, we will hire the investment banker before contacting any potential buyers on our own, so the investment banker can help us craft the story and create the right auction environment.

What's This Going to Cost Me?

Investment bankers do not get paid by the hour. Virtually all of them get paid a success fee – a commission paid only after a deal closes. Depending on the relationship and the risk of the deal, many investment bankers will request a non-refundable retainer to allow them to cover costs while they get up to speed on your company and gear up to document the story that will be told to the market. Some investment bankers will require a monthly retainer if closing a deal doesn't seem certain.

The percentage used for the success fee is negotiable. In most situations, the fee will be tiered. The investment banker may get a fee equal to 5% of the first $10 million, 4% of the amount between $10 million and $20 million, 3% of the next $10 million and so on. The use of a tiered percentage that decreases as the amount gets larger is referred to as the Lehman formula, after the old Lehman Brothers investment bank. Some investment bankers use this formula, but the market now uses a wide variety of other formulas as well.

The structure of the fee also depends on exactly what the investment banker will be doing. If the investment banker is simply serving as a financial advisor to help you get the best price from a buyer that you are already negotiating with, a flat fee might work. If the investment banker has to run a full-blown auction process for you, then the Lehman formula is probably more likely to match the investment banker's expectations.

The investment banker will offer you an engagement letter to document the economics and specify what services the investment banker will actually provide. The engagement letter for investment bankers tends to be pretty detail oriented and you will want your lawyer to review it before signing on the dotted line.

Much like the business broker, the investment banker will want to make the definition of "consideration" very clear. The consideration definition sometimes runs for an entire page. Your lawyer should guide you through each part of the definition so that you are not surprised. Most consideration paragraphs cover a wide variety of scenarios.

Investment banker engagements come in two flavors – exclusive and non-exclusive. If the engagement is exclusive, then the investment banker theoretically gives a discount off its normal success fee percentage in trade for getting credit for any buyer, whether the investment banker found the buyer or the company found the buyer on its own. If the engagement is non-exclusive, the investment banker gets its normal success fee percentage, understanding that the company could use another investment banker or find a deal through its own efforts.

The engagement letter will also contain a "tail" provision that is frequently negotiated.

As noted above in the business broker section, the investment banker is concerned about a scenario where the investment banker introduces a buyer to a seller, only to have the seller try to avoid payment by terminating the engagement with the investment banker on a Monday and selling to the buyer on a Friday. Consequently, investment bankers put in a tail provision that says that if the seller sells its business to a buyer that the investment banker contacted for the seller, regardless of what form the sale actually uses or the amount, the investment banker still gets its fee.

Virtually every investment banker will put a time limit on how long the provision applies. Normally, investment bankers get a 12 to 18 month tail period – if the seller closes a deal within 12 to 18 months after the engagement is terminated or expires, the investment banker will get paid. The tail period is negotiable.

If the engagement is non-exclusive, the seller's lawyers will encourage a seller to negotiate which buyers count and which don't. An investment banker may send a teaser to a few hundred possible buyers, some of whom don't even respond. An experienced seller will agree with the investment banker upfront – at the time of the engagement letter – on which potential buyers will be contacted. The buyers on the list will count for the tail. If the investment banker wants to suggest other possible buyers, the investment banker will only contact them once the investment banker and the seller agree to add them to the list.

At the very end of the engagement letter, you will find an exhibit in tiny print with no margins, usually entitled "Indemnification". The language is very hard to read for non-lawyers, but is required by every investment banker I have ever met. The investment banker wants to know that if a seller's shareholders, management or other constituents – or the buyer – try to sue the investment banker, that the seller will protect the investment banker. If the investment banker does something fraudulent, intentionally harmful or "grossly negligent", then the investment banker will be on its own. In all other instances, the investment banker takes the position that investment banker was just assisting the seller using the seller's information and the investment banker should be safe. Think of it as the investment banker just being the waitress – you can't be mad at her for serving food made poorly by the kitchen.

"Grossly negligent" is an important term and one that is critical to the investment banker. Everyone is negligent at some point in their lives. You are and so am I. Being grossly negligent is a different matter. Gross negligence is very hard to prove in court, while negligence in a courtroom is in the eye of the judge or jury. All investment bankers will fight like wolverines not to water down the standard to mere negligence. Experienced deal lawyers know not to touch the third rail and argue for changing the standard. Large investment banks will walk away from deals rather than go with just negligence. Argue with a good investment banker about the standard at your peril.

Conclusion

You now have a plan on who to put on our team, what role they will fill, when we need them and how to hire and pay them. Specifically, we have thought about our management team, the accountant, the lawyer and the business broker / investment banker and what each of them bring to the table. We're now ready to look at getting our house in order in the form of pre-deal due diligence.

Chapter 5: How Fast is Fast – Building the Timeline for Your Deal

What We Will Learn

This chapter will help you work out a workable timeline for getting your deal done, start to finish. We will walk through the basic elements of the deal, cheating a little by summarizing process steps that we will cover in greater detail in later chapters. We will put a range of time periods together to piece together what the timeline for our particular deal might look like.

Waiting for Godot

If you took Honors English in high school, the odds are good that you were subjected to a play by Samuel Beckett called Waiting for Godot. The play is about two guys named Vladimir and Estragon, who spend the entire play talking about a wide variety of subjects while they wait for another person named Godot. Being an absurdist play, Godot never actually shows up and the play ends. The play lasts either a few hours or a few years, I forget which.

When you are in the middle of a M&A deal, either as an owner, lawyer, accountant or employee, there are going to be numerous times when you feel like a character in the play.

As an owner, it will take longer than you want to find a buyer, unless we are dealing with an unsolicited offer or the number of potential buyers for your business is very limited. Potential buyers will express interest, and then promptly go on two week vacations. You will sign a letter of intent that says the deal will close in 60 days, but then 60 days comes and goes. The buyer promises a purchase agreement in a few days, and it arrives weeks later. The buyer's review of your business should only take 30 days, and then Day 90 arrives with more requests for information.

You must make peace with the process or you will make yourself, your team and your family crazy.

Understanding that the actual timeline will be fluid, here is an outline to set basic expectations if your business is substantial and there is time to do an orderly auction:

- Day 1 – Owner makes the decision to sell

- Days 2-15 – Owner puts together deal team
  - Employees who absolutely need to know
  - Accountant, lawyer, investment banker / broker need to be identified, interviewed and retained

- Days 15-30
  - Team goes through the business to organize documents a buyer will want to see
    - Clean up of festering issues begins (minute book or stock certificates are missing, tax returns are all on extension, financial projections only available in crayon, owner loans need to be repaid, dead accounts receivable written off)
  - List of prospective buyers put together
  - Work starts on creating a story about why the business is being sold, what the value proposition is (sell entire business? Just technology? "Acqui-hire" of our team if we have no real product or customers yet?)

49

- Possibly crank out a short "teaser" document to test the waters with potential buyers
  - o Initial research on valuations of businesses like this one

- Days 30-60
  - o If there is time and an investment banker / broker is involved, build a confidential information memorandum, telling the story
  - o Send out non-disclosure documents to interested buyers

- Days 60-90
  - o Allow serious buyers to review high level financial information, tax returns, redacted customer and vendor data
  - o Solicit offers

- Days 90-120
  - o Negotiate formal offers – letters of intent

- Day 120
  - o Sign letter of intent with best buyer, enter period where we can only negotiate with that buyer (exclusivity)

- Days 120-180
  - o Heavy review of business by buyer (due diligence)
  - o Review and negotiate purchase agreement
  - o Review and negotiate employment agreement or short-term consulting agreement for owners

- Days 180-210
  - Sign purchase agreement
  - Start working on getting consents from landlord, customers and vendors who have contracts requiring consent

- Day 210
  - All other documents are signed
  - Payment of initial purchase price
  - Press release
  - Announcement to employees
  - Calls to customers

- One year after the closing
  - If we agreed to a delayed payment (earnout), payment arrives

- 12-24 months after closing
  - If buyer has claims for losses, buyer asks for indemnification payments from owner back to buyer

- Two years after the closing
  - If we agreed to more than one delayed payment, the second earnout payment arrives

- Two to five years after the closing
  - If we agreed to a non-compete, the owners can now start a new, similar business or join a competitor

Tools to Help Yourself Manage the Process

If you use an investment banker, it's reasonable to request a timeline, either in PowerPoint form or a basic chart. You should request the timeline as you are interviewing bankers so that you know their assumptions (which are of course subject to obvious caveats) about how the process will work before you put your money down.

Once you actually have a signed letter of intent with a buyer, you can request something similar from your lawyer to cover getting the deal done. On large deals, lawyers will use a time and responsibility schedule, sometimes called a T&R chart for short. The chart is geared toward making it clear on all sides who is committed to each task and how long they have to complete it. Schedules slip for good reasons, but the T&R chart can be a useful way to apply subconscious pressure on each player to pull their weight. For smaller deals, it might not be worth the expense – it's a judgment call.

Sometimes a closing checklist, which is a different animal we will describe later, can serve a similar purpose.

Weekly "touch base" calls are also useful for seeing where logjams are appearing. The key is to set a time limit for each call to keep the calls efficient and cost-effective.

Conclusion

By thinking about the timeline tasks and the assumptions involved in giving each task the right amount of time, you should have a good sense for how much time your particular deal may take. Now we are ready to get into the details of getting ourselves ready for the dating world and meeting a qualified buyer.

Chapter 6: Getting Our House in Order: Pre-Sale Clean Up and Organizing Diligence Materials

What We Will Learn

This chapter is geared toward helping you get the most value for your business. If we think like a buyer in advance of selling our business, we may be able to eliminate or at least improve things that buyers can use as excuses to lower the price they pay for your business. We also want to start gathering documents that buyers will inevitably want to see and organize them while we have time. This exercise will save us time and money when we are ready to seek out buyers.

Let's Make Mountains into Molehills

Running a business is hard. Management will be focused on solving day to day problems and growing the business. Keeping up on minute books and organizing contract files is important, but revenue usually comes first. Having perfect files is a great aspiration.

However, when you make the decision to sell your business, you will have to start thinking like a buyer instead of an operator.

Yes, think like a buyer even though you are the seller.

Think about what a buyer will want to ask about your business.

The buyer will want to see your financial statements and tax returns. If the books are a mess, this would be the time to fix them.

If the tax returns are not filed, this would be the time to get off extension and finish them.

A buyer will want to go through your customer contracts. If we have undocumented deals or are missing amendments, we should fix those issues now.

If you have informal arrangements with your sales team on commissions, this would be the time to document them or replace them with something consistent across the team.

The buyer's legal and accounting teams will need to conduct due diligence on your business, reviewing all of the company's records. In principle, they are looking for liabilities and to prove that the assets, contracts and intellectual property that you say are valuable actually exist and match the story you have to tell.

These teams are also looking to give the buyer material to use to possibly argue that the purchase prices should be lowered after you have started a deal.

Knowing this, you should identify the problems with your business and your records and clean them up now. The hard work you put in now to clean up your house will literally save you money once the deal starts.

Getting Organized – Preparation for Due Diligence

Most buyers will want to review your business records in an organized fashion. The process is referred to as "due diligence" – the phrase is meant to convey that a smart buyer will be reasonably diligent in reviewing a seller's records before writing a check.

You can expect that the buyer will present you with a due diligence checklist. Sometimes the checklist is short, sometimes it goes on for 20-25 pages, based on the size of your business and the buyer's experiences with other deals.

In anticipation of getting a due diligence checklist, a smart seller will ask its own advisors for a due diligence checklist. Then, the seller can organize all of the documents that a buyer is likely to request and be ready for them.

How Much Information is Too Much Information?

If this is your first time selling a business, you may have fears about how much information to share with a buyer. Isn't the buyer just looking for reasons to lower the price? If I tell them about bad things, don't I risk losing the buyer? Can't we just tell them later, or pray that they don't find the problem?

Prospective buyers do a diligence review for a number of reasons.

Sure, buyers are looking for liabilities or flaws that may allow them to argue for a price reduction. However, the good ones will really want to buy the business not because they are getting an asset for a discount, but because your business could add substantial value to their existing business. Not everyone is looking to nickel and dime you.

Buyers are also looking to confirm for their masters that the business is healthy and worth the money. If I am the head of business development for a Fortune 500 company, I cannot afford to report to my CEO two years after our purchase of your business that the business is now worth 50% of what we paid. The CEO will not want to report that to her board. As the buyer, diligence is also CYA or protecting your career and your business.

Buyers also want to make sure that they know early on where they will have to put in extra effort into integrating your employees, vendors and customers into their existing empire. If your engineers are better than the buyer's engineers, they may choose to replace some theirs with some of yours. If your databases are run on outdated software, the buyer may not lower the purchase price, but the buyer's IT staff will need to start thinking now about how to migrate your database to their platform. Some of the diligence is just practical preparation.

What if your business really does have a serious problem, like environmental liability or a lawsuit that isn't going well?

Most buyers will not purchase your business "as is". The buyer will want you to make promises about the state of the business in the purchase agreement. These promises are called "representations and warranties", which we will cover in a later chapter. If the promises you make are not correct, the buyer will make sure that the buyer can either get some of its money back or simply cut back or eliminate payments to be made in the future if some of the purchase price is deferred. The buyer will place these promises into different categories with respect to how long they can hold you to them:

- For "fundamental representations" like whether you actually owned the stock you just sold to the buyer or whether the company actually existed, you may be expected to back up the promise indefinitely.

- For "statutory representations" like taxes, regulatory or environmental matters where you would have been on the hook for a period of time tied to a statute of limitations, the buyer will want you to be on the hook for that period of time.

- For "general representations" like whether your customer list was accurate or whether you listed all material contracts, the buyer may want you to back up the promise for a period between 12 to 36 months.

The buyer sets these time frames to match the severity of a potential broken promise to the buyer economically and to the odds that a broken promise won't surface before the period runs out.

Given the length of time that the promises will last, the question you have to answer is whether you would like to disclose a problem now, with the story you want to tell about the actual severity and possible fixes, or wait until the buyer discovers it on its own and comes back to you really angry.

The Data Room

Back in the day, a seller's law firm would organize a "data room", which would be an actual conference room with boxes and boxes of the seller's documents. The buyer's diligence team would be invited to physically come to the data room and would be supervised while they spent hours or days summarizing all of the materials that the seller provided.

These days, deal advisors will refer to a "virtual data room." The seller's advisors will use a cloud provider like Interlinks or Merrill to host a server where all of the seller's documents will be uploaded and available for review by prospective buyers. The seller's advisors will be able to control which prospective buyers see which documents and at what point in the process they can see a given document. The virtual data room also allows the seller's advisors to see who is actually looking at documents and for how long – this is important because if Buyer A only looks at five documents for 10 minutes and Buyer B looks at the entire data room using multiple team members for significant periods of time – guess which one is likely to be the more serious buyer?

The virtual data room will be organized into folders.

You can expect to upload documents in the following categories:

- Corporate records
  - Articles, bylaws, minute books
  - Stock ledger
  - Copies of warrants, stock options, other securities
- Financial records
  - Income statement
  - Balance sheet
  - Cash flow statement
  - Tax returns
  - Budgets
  - Projections
  - Accounts payable
  - Accounts receivables
  - Loans
  - Guarantees
  - Liens
- Contracts
  - Customer agreements
    - Top 20 customers by revenue
  - Vendor agreements
    - Top 20 vendors by expense
  - Equipment leases
  - Office leases
- Intellectual Property
  - Patents, copyrights, trademarks
  - Software licenses
  - Employee confidentiality agreements
- HR
  - Employment agreements
  - Offer letters
  - Headcount and salary information

- o Benefit plans
- o Employee manuals
- Litigation
- Real estate and environmental issues
- Insurance

Advanced Cleanup

Now that you have thought about the categories of documents you will need to provide, let's do a second, deeper dive into getting our house in order.

In addition to fixing problems, let's think about enhancing the value of what we have, too.

If you have customer agreements that are about to expire, this might be a good time to try to get extensions so a future buyer doesn't discount the revenue we have.

If we have only one vendor providing our only source of a key component to what we do, this would be an excellent time to go find a second supplier so a future buyer doesn't claim that our business is at risk if the vendor doesn't want to do business with our company after the new buyer shows up.

You will want to take a look at your balance sheet to see if there are items that were fine when you owned the business but will confuse a potential buyer. If there is a "company condo" or private jet, this would be the time to remove them.

Thinking of ways to add value to what we already have may not only help us avoid a price reduction, but may actually help us get an even better offer in the first place.

Cleanup, Part Three – Minute Books

If you have not kept up with your minute books or have issued stock without a corresponding board consent, I would encourage you not to "recreate" them. At best, prospective buyers might view "recreated" minutes as a sign of sloppiness, at worst, you might end up looking like you did something inching toward fraud.

The better practice is to look at what material actions have been taken in the past and have the board, and the shareholders if appropriate, pass resolutions that ratify the prior actions.

Cleanup, Part Four – Intellectual Property

You may have put off filing for a registered trademark because you did not want to spend $1,000 to get the filing done. You may have a provisional patent that you never finished due to the expense. You will want to think like a buyer of your business and determine whether spending a few dollars improving the defensibility of your intellectual property will be worth a significant bump in your ultimate purchase price.

Cleanup, Part Four – Literally Cleaning Up

Before you start showing potential buyers around your office or manufacturing plant, you will want to pay a few bucks for fresh paint. If you have old equipment or things that detract from the image you want to present, removing them now will serve you well.

Conclusion

In this chapter, we focused on reducing opportunities for a buyer to lower our purchase price by cleaning up sore spots in our business. We know the collection of documents we need to gather, how to organize them and the benefit of using a virtual data room.

We also have thought about some advanced techniques to create additional value before we go out to market.

Chapter 7: Running an Auction

What We Will Learn

This chapter will focus on how to sell your business using an auction process. We will discuss the pros and cons of using an auction. Then we will go through the process hinted at in the timeline in Chapter 5 in greater detail.

The Value of An Auction Process

There are a wide variety of ways to place a value on your business. There are simple methods, like using the value of comparable companies – find a few companies that look like yours and see what their sale prices were. There are complex methods, like discounted cash flow analysis, where we figure out the value of your business's ability to generate cash based on educated guesses on whether your business will grow or shrink, with an appropriate discount rate being applied.

Ultimately, a business is worth what someone is willing to pay for it. If you only approach one buyer, or go with the first buyer to approach you, then you may end up wondering if you could have received a better deal if other bidders were at the table.

From an economic perspective, the best way to figure out the value of your business is to ask the marketplace. If you put the business up for sale in an auction, then the market will tell you what the best price is.

Conducting an auction almost always requires using an investment banker (or a business broker for smaller deals).

As we discussed in Chapter 4, an investment banker is a specialist, involved in buying and selling businesses, along with raising debt and equity funds for businesses.

Once you have engaged an investment banker, the investment banker will work with you to put together a list of potential auction participants. The investment banker will think about whether strategic buyers or financial buyers are right for the business. The investment banker will also talk with you about your goals (i.e., retirement, working for a potential buyer, what happens to the employees, etc.).

The investment banker will review the business's financial statements and projections to help you set expectations on how much the business may ultimately receive as a purchase price. The investment banker may use a variety of models to come up with a range of values. While you will not volunteer the models or the range of prices to potential buyers, the models will be very useful when it comes time to negotiate with buyers on why they should raise their offers.

The investment banker will then develop a teaser to start an auction. The teaser document usually is a description of the company that will be used to get potential buyers interested enough to ask for a second, more detailed document. The teaser will typically not include the company's name.

When potential buyers indicate that they would like to know more, the investment banker will offer to provide them with the detailed document, after the potential buyers sign a non-disclosure agreement.

The non-disclosure agreement is different than the document you might use with a new customer or vendor. This version protects not only the information you will be sharing with potential buyers, but also is intended to keep the sales discussions themselves, and the fact that the business is up for sale, which itself should be confidential.

Once potential buyers sign the non-disclosure agreement, or NDA for short, the investment banker will provide a sales document called a confidential information memorandum to the potential buyers. This document will go through the company's history, product offerings, management team biographies, basic financial information and other information that a buyer is likely to request. The document is frequently provided with disclaimers, making it clear that potential buyers will have to rely on their own investigation of the business and are not supposed to hold the seller liable for what is said in the memorandum, assuming the seller hasn't said something knowingly false.

Next, the investment banker will either allow some limited diligence review of very basic documents from the seller, or will request a letter right then from potential buyers called an indication of interest. The buyer's indication of interest will give a range of prices the buyer may be willing to pay, tell the seller how fast the buyer can move, and explain whether the buyer has the financing it needs to do the deal.

The investment banker will help the seller sort through the indications of interest and select the potential buyers that should be allowed to go to the next round.

Auction participants that make the cut will then be allowed to review a much more detailed level of information about the seller's company, with the expectation that the buyers will then make a specific offer after they have finished their review.

In Chapter 6, we discussed the use of virtual data rooms. While most M&A advisors have drunk the Kool-Aid and regularly use virtual data rooms for the convenience they offer, occasionally having an actual conference room with paper documents isn't a bad thing.

If you are lucky and have an active auction on your hands, using an actual conference room can force prospective buyers to have to start and finish their diligence in a compressed timeframe. When you use a virtual data room, multiple buyers can look at the diligence at once and can take their time in reviewing what you have. With a real data room, the seller will only allow one buyer in the room at a time so the bidders don't know who the other bidders are. This means, that Bidder A may only get three days in the room, to make time available for Bidders B and C to also get three days to themselves. Practically, this means that Bidder A has to do all of its diligence in three days – it can't putter around, taking weeks to review the seller's materials.

That being said, most sellers will go with virtual data rooms and just try to be disciplined on how long they will allow "virtual" diligence to continue.

Investment bankers will have different theories on when they would like buyers to interact with the seller's management team. The most senior managers will likely be asked to give a presentation at some point during the process, usually as close to the end of the process as the auction will allow.

Additional Preparation for the Auction – Retaining Management

Auctions can be scary, not just for the owners, but for management as well if the company is substantial. Before initiating an auction, the owners will want to identify management team members who are key to the business from a buyer's perspective, as well as managers that will be asked to actively participate in the auction process.

It's important to remember that managers will have reasonable concerns about not only which buyers may be good for the business, but also which buyers may be best for them personally. The more time a manager gets to spend with a particular buyer's diligence team, the more opportunities that manager has to steer the deal toward a buyer who is more likely to keep that manager after the deal.

Smart sellers will offer a retention bonus to key team members who are willing to stay through the entire auction. The bonus will motivate them not to start a job hunt (or at least take a new job) until after the auction is complete.

The seller may also craft the retention bonus to be paid after a period of time has gone by after the sale, to motivate the team member not to immediately defect after the sale if that team member is going to be important to the buyer.

Diligencing the Buyers

While the auction is running, the seller's team should also do some basic investigation of the buyers as well. The seller's team should send a due diligence request list of its own, asking for key information to be provided to the seller by the buyer.

Before accepting an offer, the seller should know if the buyer has the funds to actually close the deal. If the buyer is relying on bank financing, we will want to know that the buyer's bank is committed to make the loan.

If the buyer is likely to propose paying some of the purchase price now, and some of the purchase price later (i.e., an "earnout" discussed in Chapter 10, you should see if there is any information on how often the buyer ends up refusing to pay later amounts. A great way to check on the buyer's history is to see if they have done prior acquisitions and try to speak with the sellers in those deals, understanding that the sellers may have contractual obligations not to make negative statements about the buyer – you may have to read between the lines in your discussions with them.

If the buyer is going to propose using its stock instead of just cash, you need to view taking buyer stock as the same as making an investment of our cash in the buyer.

We should find out how healthy the buyer's business is. If the buyer's stock is not publicly traded, you will want assurances you will be able to sell the stock. You may also want to quietly run a criminal background check on the buyer's senior management if we are going to be taking their stock.

We should also try to understand what each buyer's motivation is in participating in the auction. If a particular buyer thinks that our products will help make selling their own products easier, or buying our plant allows the buyer to close a plant elsewhere, we should emphasize these factors when discussing price.

The more intelligence you can gather on potential buyers before actual bids are made, the better your position will be when trying to evaluate the bids.

Staying Connected

The lead person for the seller's team should make sure to keep the team organized and informed during the process.

It's very important that anyone interacting with the buyers understands what everyone else is saying to them. Having different players contradict each other cannot possibly help you get the best price. Weekly conference calls can reduce the risk of mixed communications. If you are worried about runaway conference calls, setting a call length in advance and distributing a short agenda before each call can help corral your team and keep the calls efficient.

Conclusion

We have learned the benefits of using an auction to locate buyers and accept bids. We now understand the components of an auction. We learned reasons why we should probably investigate basic facts about the auction participants. We also thought about how to keep our team connected during the process. Now we are ready to start thinking about deal structures.

Chapter 8: The Letter of Intent

What We Will Learn

In this chapter, we are going to look at the first major document to be negotiated – the letter of intent. We will discuss the purpose of a letter of intent. We will review what elements should be binding and what should be non-binding. We will also discuss negotiating tactics that come into play at this stage.

Why Letters of Intent are Used

When a buyer is ready to make its offer, the buyer will want to know that the seller is on the same page before the buyer spends money on advisors and valuable management time pursuing the seller. Many buyers will use a letter of intent as the mechanism to make sure the parties are in basic agreement on the most fundamental deal terms.

The letter of intent is usually delivered in the form of a letter from the buyer to the seller. The letter will serve as the skeleton for the deal. The letter will address major deal points, but won't address everything; the muscle and skin will be added when the main purchase agreement is drafted. Sometimes the purchase agreement will also be called the "definitive" agreement.

Somewhat confusingly, the document might be called:

- A letter of intent, or LOI
- A memorandum of understanding, or MOU
- A term sheet

Regardless of the term used, the document will cover the same elements.

Binding Versus Non-Binding

A good LOI has terms that the parties intend to bind them legally and other terms that are "gentleman's agreements" until the buyer has had an opportunity to perform its diligence on the seller's business.

Most deal lawyers will tell you that fully binding LOIs are almost always an invitation to litigation, since the LOI is really just a rough sketch of the deal, with the picture only becoming clear when the definitive agreement is drafted.

The economic terms of the deal like pricing, timing of payments, deal structure are usually kept non-binding. The idea is that the parties intend to honor the economic terms, but understand that if the buyer finds something wrong in the diligence or a major customer refuses to cooperate, then the economics may have to change.

The key parts of the LOI that are nearly always binding are the sections covering confidentiality and exclusivity.

Confidentiality

If the seller is approached by a buyer directly instead of through an auction, the LOI will usually contain a section requiring both parties to keep the discussion and the LOI itself confidential. Alternatively, the LOI may reference a pre-existing non-disclosure agreement if one was signed prior to the offer being made.

Non-Solicitation

If the potential buyer is a competitor or a player in the same industry as the seller, the seller may want to consider a non-solicitation clause. This provision would prohibit the buyer from directly approaching the seller's employees for employment with the buyer if the acquisition falls through. The buyer may negotiate to have such a provision only cover employees whom the buyer actually met during the process and allow for an exception for solicitations made through an advertisement as opposed to a phone call or email straight to the given employee. The seller wants to be careful not to overdo it – states like California may invalidate a provision that goes past solicitation and forbids a buyer hiring the seller's employees under any circumstances.

The non-solicitation clause could also include a prohibition on soliciting the seller's customers and vendors as well.

Exclusivity

Buyers will usually require that the seller agree not to "shop" itself to other potential buyers for a period of time. The buyer will make this request on the theory that the buyer will be paying for lawyers, accountants and other advisors to review the selling company's operations and records. The buyer doesn't want to spend the funds and the time if the seller is not serious about a potential marriage with the buyer.

The fact that exclusivity will expire after a specific date can actually serve the seller. If the buyer dawdles and takes too long on diligence, the buyer may find that the exclusivity period is about to expire. The seller can agree to extend the exclusivity, but may choose to allow the buyer to continue non-exclusive talks (meaning the seller can now court other buyers while the first buyer finishes screwing around) or extend the period for a very short period of time to motivate the buyer to finish the deal.

If the seller has leverage in the negotiations, the buyer has a reputation for not closing deals or the seller has other interested buyers, the seller may decide to agree to grant exclusivity if the buyer is willing to compensate the seller for a failed transaction with a "breakup" fee, paid if the deal doesn't close for reasons other than the seller's lack of cooperation. This term would obviously also need to be binding.

Remember that if the parties agree to extend exclusivity, they should probably also extend their respective non-disclosure obligations. The two promises should go hand in hand.

Elements of the LOI

My clients tend to use a letter of intent to communicate the binding elements (confidentiality and exclusivity), with a term sheet covering the economic deal points attached to the letter. They like this format to help bolster the argument that the economic offer really is not binding until we get to the definitive agreement.

There is always a balancing act on how much to cover at the LOI stage. If the buyer puts too much detail into the LOI, the seller may view them as a difficult buyer. If the buyer puts in too little, the parties may end up not really having a locked down structure and the definitive agreement could require longer, harder negotiation.

Typically, the LOI will at least cover:

- What is being purchased – either the assets of the business or the equity held by the owners of the business
- What the purchase price will be
- When the purchase price will be paid
- Whether the purchase price is contingent on future events
- Whether the purchase price is going to paid in cash, buyer stock, or buyer debt like promissory notes
- What tax treatment the parties want for the transaction

Most LOIs will also cover:

- Whether the seller gets to keep particular assets
- Whether the seller has to keep particular liabilities
- What happens to the seller's employees
- Whether the management team will stay on and on what terms
- Whether there are critical relationships that have to passed on like major customers, vendors
- How the seller's facilities will be handled

Generally, lawyers advise their sell-side clients that the seller's leverage starts going down as soon as the LOI is signed. Once the parties agree on the price and the structure, the price can only go down from there, as the buyer finds issues in the diligence. Consequently, it sometimes serves the seller to include key points (from the seller's perspective) that are not addressed in the buyer's version. For example, if the seller's CEO is supposed to stay after the closing, the LOI may address the CEO's salary, benefits and perks after the acquisition. The LOI may also lay out when the buyer can no longer ask for its money back due to liabilities that surface after the closing.

Negotiating Tactics

The letter of intent will contain a "drop dead" date. The LOI will state that the offer in the LOI is only good until a specific date. If the seller accepts the offer after the date, the buyer is no longer obligated to do the deal on the terms in the LOI, even on a gentleman's agreement level.

The existence of a drop dead date doesn't always mean that the buyer will truly walk away. Many times, the drop dead date is the only way that a buyer can motivate a seller to give some kind of response. The actual negotiation of the LOI can go on for some time, depending on the parties' motivations.

After the LOI is signed, sometimes parties will have fascinating views of the gentleman's agreement element. I have seen sellers sign a LOI and then as soon as they see the definitive agreement draft, the sellers will try to toss out concepts clearly covered in the LOI. These sellers will argue that the LOI was non-binding, so they can renegotiate whatever they wish.

While they are technically correct, sellers that behave this way are inviting the buyer to unscramble the egg on what the buyer was willing to pay too, so playing games like this can be a dangerous proposition.

Conclusion

Reading this chapter, you have now learned:

- Why LOIs are used
- The importance of separating binding elements from non-binding elements
- Key points to include
- Key negotiating tips

Now we are ready to consider what types of structures are available for our deal.

Chapter 9: Deal Structures

What We Will Learn

In this chapter, we will learn about the different structures that a buyer may propose when offering to buy a business. We will look at the upside and downside to each structure from the buyer's perspective, to understand better why they may propose the given structure. Then we will review the upside and downside to the seller so we understand the effect on the seller.

The Asset Purchase

Most buyers will prefer to buy the assets of a seller's business rather than the stock or other equity owned by the seller.

Upside for the Buyer

The buyer likes an asset deal for a number of reasons.

Skipping Overvalued Assets

First, the buyer will be able to pick the assets that are valuable to the buyer, and leave behind assets that the buyer sees as less valuable.

Why would the buyer not want all of the assets?

The best example probably is accounts receivable. Accounts receivable is the money owed to a business by its customers that hasn't been actually received yet.

If the business is owed $250,000 and all of the accounts receivable is due within 30 days, the accounts receivable is probably worth $250,000.

If the accounts receivable equals a total of $250,000, but $200,000 has been due for over a year, the odds are probably high that the $200,000 is never going to get paid.

From the seller's perspective, the accounts receivable might be worth $250,000. The buyer thinks the accounts receivable is really worth $50,000 after writing off the other $200,000 basically uncollectible. The buyer may be willing to pay for the "good" accounts receivable, but doesn't want to pay much of anything for the rest. Rather than argue, the buyer may just tell the seller to keep the accounts receivable and not pay for it.

Avoiding Liabilities

The buyer also likes an asset deal because it can buy the components of the business and leave a number of the liabilities still inside the acquired company (or "target" company), for the seller to deal with after the deal.

The buyer will consider three types of liabilities.

First, there are liabilities that the buyer either cannot avoid or wants to actually accept or "assume". The building lease may be worth accepting if the buyer needs the facility. Vendor contracts could be worth assuming if the company had a good deal or the vendor was critical.

Second, there are liabilities that the buyer can identify but does not want to assume. The owner / CEO's car lease won't interest the buyer if the owner is not going to stay with the business after the deal. A contracts with a vendor where the buyer also has a contract with the same vendor but on more favorable terms may not be worth taking.

Lastly, there are liabilities that the buyer cannot identify and does not want. Even after due diligence, claims against the company may show up only after the buyer has bought the business, like warranty claims arising from sales made before the closing. The buyer can avoid being hit with these liabilities by doing an asset purchase.

Tax Benefits

Depending on the industry, the buyer may want to get the benefit of a "step up in basis" for the acquired company's assets.

In English, if the target company bought punch press machinery for a factory ten years ago, the tax basis of the asset would decrease over time for tax purposes. The business would have taken deductions on its taxes for the decreasing value of the machinery – this is called "depreciation."

If the buyer comes along and buys the business using an asset structure, it can spread the purchase price across the assets and increase the tax basis in the assets. Now the buyer can get fresh depreciation write-offs. Depending on the equipment and the price, the tax savings could be substantial for the buyer. The process of spreading the purchase price over the asset categories is called "purchase price allocation".

Downside for the Buyer

Economically, there are few if any downsides for the buyer using an asset structure, other than understanding that if the target company is selling tangible assets to the buyer, the seller is obligated to collect sales tax on that portion of the sale.

There are logistical downsides, though.

The acquired company's contracts are assets. In an asset deal, the buyer will have to "buy" the contracts. From a practical standpoint, this means that the buyer and seller may have to go to customers, vendors, the landlord, etc. and ask the other parties to consent to the transfer of contracts from the company to the buyer. This process usually takes some time, even when the other party to a contract is cooperative. Sometimes a request for a consent to assignment is made, the other party will view it as an invitation to renegotiate or cancel a contract. These potential outcomes put the buyer at risk that the buyer could lose key contracts during the deal or at best have a slower process than it might like. Normally the upside benefits trump the contract assignment concerns, but not always.

The Seller Won't Sell

If the seller has multiple suitors, the buyer offering to do an asset deal may lose out to a buyer offering a more favorable structure to the seller. The buyer could lose the deal before it even starts.

The buyer proposing an asset deal might also be asking the seller to take a potentially significant tax hit. If the seller has only one dance partner, the buyer may be in a position to impose the structure. The buyer may also offer a higher purchase price to get the asset structure it wants, but offering the asset purchase structure may lengthen the negotiations at the letter of intent stage.

Upside for the Seller

A seller normally doesn't like the tax implications of an asset sale, but there are some good reasons why a seller might like the structure.

Selling One Business Line or Division

If the target company has a few different lines of business being run out of the same company, the seller may not want to sell its stock. Instead, the target may want to just get rid of one business line. In situations like this, an asset sale may be best.

Retaining a Valuable Asset

If the acquired company owns real estate in addition to operating assets, the seller may prefer to keep the real estate and sell off the business, especially where potential buyers are unlikely to want the real estate or might undervalue the property.

The Seller Can Handle Liabilities Better than the Buyer

Sometimes the acquired company will have flaws. The seller and the buyer both know what the flaws are. The seller may believe it can address the flaws more effectively than the buyer.

Imagine the target company had a lawsuit over a customer contract. The seller thinks it can handle the suit and settle for $50,000. The buyer has no idea what the lawsuit might ultimately cost and is concerned the buyer could be on the hook for hundreds of thousands of dollars if the case goes badly. The buyer is willing to handle the suit but wants the seller to cover the cost, regardless of how much the bill ends up being. The buyer agrees to assume the suit if the buyer can hold back a significant part of the purchase price until after the suit is settled. The seller may decide to sell the company's assets and just retain the lawsuit rather than sell stock and have part of the purchase price be at risk.

Downside for the Seller

Taxes, Taxes, Taxes

If the target company is a "C corporation" for tax purposes or recently made an "S corporation" tax election, the biggest disadvantage for the seller is the tax impact. When the target company sells its assets, the company will have to pay taxes.

After the deal, the company will have few if any assets other than cash paid by the buyer.

The company will pay off its creditors, using the cash left over after paying the company level taxes.

Then, when the sellers cause the company to distribute the remaining cash, the sellers will have to pay tax again on the distributions.

Depending on the transaction, the ultimate tax hit could range from 55-60% for a C corporation selling its assets in California to 30-33% if the company selling its assets is an S corporation or LLC. See Appendix A for a few examples.

Chasing Minority Shareholders if the Buyer Makes a Post-Closing Claim

When a buyer purchases the assets of a target company, the owners of the company may elect to dissolve the company after the deal closes.

However, the buyer knows that even though it didn't assume most of the company's liabilities, there may still be problems with what the buyer purchased. The buyer will want to make sure that the buyer can go back to the seller, sometimes a few years later, to ask for money back if the buyer suffered losses from the seller's broken promises. We covered these promises, called representations and warranties, in Chapter 6, along with the time periods that buyers expect to have to recover losses.

If the company is owned by a number of shareholders, the buyer may ask that all of the shareholders agree to be liable for the entire amount of any loss, on the theory that the shareholders are better positioned to chase each other for their fair shares of the loss, rather than having the buyer go through the headache of chasing each of them individually. This is called "joint and several liability".

The practical implication for the sellers is that the buyer could hand the loss to one large shareholder and expect that shareholder to either pay the loss or go chase his fellow shareholders on his own.

The Stock Purchase

In a stock purchase transaction, the buyer will purchase the stock or other equity owned by the owners of the target company. Rather than change anything inside the company, the company will just end up with new owners at the end of the deal.

Upside for the Buyer

As noted above, the buyer may propose (or ultimately agree to) a stock deal where there are contract consents that will make a deal move too slowly.

Understand that there may still be consents to assignment required even in a stock deal where the owners change but the business remains the same. Frequently, the lease's assignment clause require consent whether the contract is "assigned" in an asset transfer or a "change of control" is deemed to occur in a stock transaction. The landlord may specifically include language that states that any transfer of the lease resulting from a change of control in the ownership of the company greater than XX% will require the landlord's consent. Other contracts may have similar provisions.

The buyer may also use a stock purchase structure when there are licenses or regulatory permits involved, based on the same "assignment" versus "change of control" analysis.

The buyer may also not want to lose out to other bidders in an auction, as noted previously.

Downside for the Buyer

The buyer of the target company's stock will now be taking the entire company, with all of its liabilities, whether known or unknown. The buyer will be at risk of getting surprised. The buyer will also be at risk of paying catastrophic losses where the liability of the selling shareholders is capped at $X but the actual losses exceed the purchase price. If the company owned oil wells that caused contamination, the losses caused by environmental damage could exceed the actual purchase price for the business. Buyer management teams get fired for those kinds of things.

Theoretically, the buyer may also lose the benefit of the step up in basis on the target company's assets discussed above. However, the federal tax code gives buyers mechanisms called Section 336(e) or 338(h)(10) elections to recapture the lost basis. The sellers might have an increase in their tax liability if they agree to let the buyer use the election, but frequently buyers will be willing to increase, or "gross up", the purchase price to offset the sellers' tax liability from "depreciation recapture" where the benefit to the buyers is greater than the hit to the sellers. The elections are issues that are properly addressed during the LOI stage.

Upside for the Seller

The seller likes a stock sale for a variety of reasons.

First, the seller avoids the double taxation that might result from an asset sale for some sellers.

Second, the seller no longer has to worry about spending time and money after the closing to wind up the business and deal with creditors and distribution payments.

Third, while the seller may still be on the hook for losses arising from breaches of representations and warranties for a while, the seller no longer has to live with the day to day issues coming from handling retained liabilities on his own.

Downside to the Seller

The seller may end up with a lower purchase price by insisting on a stock sale.

Even with a stock purchase structure, companies with multiple shareholders will still likely have the issue of dealing with joint and several liability, as discussed above.

The "Stock Swap" or Merger

In larger transactions, a buyer may want to acquire a business in the form of a merger.

There are a variety of forms of mergers, some of which get quite complicated. Usually the form and number of entities involved are guided by the desire to eliminate or at least limit the taxes payable by the seller in the transaction.

In its simplest form, a merger could just involve the company merging into the buyer. When the merger is completed, the company disappears and all that is left is the buyer entity. The merger will involve a trade: the buyer trades cash or stock for the selling shareholder's equity.

If the target company has great contracts or key licenses, the buyer may actually merge into the seller.

Sometimes, mergers will take more complex forms. The buyer may form a subsidiary that will merge with the company. These transactions are called triangular mergers.

Rather than get lost in the details and tax implications of triangular mergers, we are going to focus instead on the upsides and downsides to mergers generally.

Upside for the Buyer

Mergers have a few benefits to the buyer.

Using Equity to Pay the Purchase Price

Selling shareholders may like getting buyer stock in a merger because frequently the sellers don't pay any tax by taking the buyer's stock. Effectively, the sellers are just trading one set of shares for another set of shares, so the tax authorities don't view it as cashing out on the original stock investment by the sellers. If a buyer believes that its stock is prized by sellers as an asset that is going to appreciate in value, the buyer may be able to conserve its cash to use for other needs and just use its stock to do acquisitions.

Keeping Financial Statements and Liabilities Separate

If the buyer uses a merger subsidiary to merge into the target company, the buyer can still keep the newly combined company as a separate entity for financial statements, which it would not be able to do if the buyer acquired the target company's assets.

Similarly, the buyer could use the merger subsidiary to keep the target company's liabilities sealed off in the newly combined company, instead of absorbing the liabilities into its existing entity.

Downside for the Buyer

Mergers can be complicated beasts, especially from a tax structuring side. Doing a merger may involve legal and accounting costs that a buyer may not want to incur for a smaller deal.

Mergers can use either cash or stock as consideration, but using stock typically has a greater tax benefit. However, the buyer may not want to use its stock to buy the target company.

The buyer may view its stock as undervalued. The buyer may not want the dilution that comes from the buying entity having to issue more shares to do the acquisition. For these reasons, the buyer may rather just use cash to buy the target company, even if the buyer has to borrow money.

Upside for the Seller

If the buyer is using its equity to buy the target company in the merger, the seller may get significant tax savings. The seller also gets the benefit of walking away from having to wind up the target company, much like a stock sale.

The consent process can also be easier, since assignment provisions in contracts frequently require consents in asset or stock sales, but may not cover "transfers by operation of law" – which include mergers. Licenses and permits can similarly be easier to transfer to a buyer in a merger than in one of the alternative structures.

Downside for the Seller

Mergers are not always tax-free for a seller. If a buyer uses a mix of buyer stock and cash, the cash component can be viewed by tax authorities as "boot" – taxable proceeds from the sale. If there is too much "boot", the tax-free benefits for the stock portion of the consideration can get blown out. Tax lawyers have to watch the mix of consideration very carefully in mergers using both cash and stock.

Sellers also need to consider how long they will have to hold the buyer's stock. If the buyer is public, the seller may be able to sell some of the stock in the marketplace after a period of time. If the buyer is private, the seller may have to hold the buyer's stock for an indefinite period of time. This can be unnerving where the buyer's stock now constitutes a large portion of the seller's net worth; the seller may be better off just taking cash and investing in a more diversified portfolio of stock, real estate and other assets.

The Exclusive License

For technology driven companies, sometimes a buyer will leave the target company standing, and just license the company's technology on an exclusive basis. These deals are trickier from a variety of standpoints, including tax, liability and other areas, but if the only core asset inside the target company is intellectual property, the exclusive license is a mechanism that a buyer may propose.

Conclusion

By working through this chapter, you have now learned the upsides and downsides for each party in a variety of purchase structures, including asset purchases, stock purchases, mergers and exclusive licenses.

We are now ready to walk through what an actual purchase agreement looks like.

Chapter 10: The Purchase Agreement

What We Will Learn

In this chapter, we are going to de-mystify the most important document in any deal – the purchase agreement. We will go through each major section and spend extra time on some of the trickier provisions. Our goal is to give you the ability to have enough knowledge to give guidance to your lawyer on what you care about and what you are willing to trade.

The Definitive Agreement

In any transaction, the primary document for the sale of a business is called the "definitive agreement". If you are selling stock or assets, the definitive agreement will be called the stock purchase agreement or the asset purchase agreement. In a merger, whether the merger involves just the buyer and seller, or the buyer, a subsidiary and the seller, the definitive agreement will be called the merger agreement.

All of the other documents involved in the deal are usually referenced in the definitive agreement. For the sake of keeping things simple, this chapter will just use the term "purchase agreement".

Unless the seller has multiple interested buyers and can impose its own form of purchase agreement on them, the buyer's lawyers will almost always draft the purchase agreement. The buyer wants to make sure that the buyer has covered all of the bases laid out in the letter of intent and that if there is an issue of interpretation, that the initial purchase agreement is not biased against the buyer.

The purchase agreement will be divided in to key sections:

- Definitions
- Purchase and sale terms and deliverables
- Closing Mechanics and Termination
- Seller representations and warranties
- Buyer representations and warranties
- Pre-closing promises or "covenants"
- Post-closing covenants
- Closing Conditions
- Indemnification
- "Miscellaneous" clauses
- Signature pages
- Exhibits
- Schedules

Some of these sections sound really boring or obvious, but it's the "boilerplate" sections that contain other people's sorry life lessons, so we are going to highlight key areas in the boilerplate too that we want sellers to understand.

Definitions – Why You Care

Right away we are going to start with a section that seems obvious but can contain traps for the unwary – the definition section.

While this may seem like a section that only a lawyer could love, some of the definitions have major consequences on how key parts of the document work.

If you are buying a very small business, the purchase agreement may not have a separate definition section. Most deals worth $2-3 million or more will typically start with a definition section that can run for several pages.

"Knowledge" and "Key Employees" are terms that sellers should read carefully. Knowledge is used to qualify promises that the seller is making about its business. As an example, the seller should be able to say whether or not the target company is currently involved in any litigation. However, the seller may not know with 100% certainty whether there are any threatened lawsuits. Maybe a complaint was filed with the court yesterday but hasn't been served on the target company's management yet. In a situation like this, the seller will request to change the litigation representation covering threatened lawsuits to say it has "no knowledge" of threatened lawsuits.

As to what "knowledge" means, parties can disagree, so they have to include a definition. Does knowledge mean facts that the CEO knows? The CEO and the CFO? The CEO, CFO and the receptionist? Normally, the definition is drafted to cover knowledge of a specific group of target company personnel. The agreement might list the group in another definition – "key employees".

Sometimes, definitions are used for multiple purposes. The same group of people that should have "knowledge" might also be the folks that a buyer really needs to stay after the deal closes. Using this example, "Key employee" could be used for two or more different purposes.

Definitions may also include specific lists that are important to the seller. As an example, in a sale of the target company's assets, the target company may get to keep "Excluded Assets". Normally, the definition will simply refer to a schedule listing the assets to be retained, but if the list is short, the list may just end up in the definition. If the selling business owner glides by the definition in her review of the agreement, she may not look hard enough at the definition to realize that there are more assets she wants to exclude than what the definition incorporates.

Similarly, looking hard at the "Excluded Liabilities" definition may find things that the buyer's lawyer thought were standard in any deal but do not apply to the particular transaction in front of the seller.

Believe it or not, what kind of day we mean can also be important in the purchase agreement. Do we mean calendar day – Monday through Sunday? Or do we mean business day – Monday through Friday? Do we mean business day in Los Angeles, or business day in Tel Aviv, where they have very different holidays than in Los Angeles? Usually "day" is important in figuring out when payments are due to the seller or how many days the buyer has to make an indemnification claim, so getting the meaning of "day" right can be important.

Purchase and Sale Section

While most sellers actually read the purchase and sale section, we are now going to go through what to look for, beyond whether the dollar amounts are correct.

Form of Transaction

The purchase and sale section makes it clear what the buyer is actually purchasing and what the buyer is not taking. The first section in an asset deal will state that the buyer is buying the target company's assets, minus excluded liabilities and excluded assets. In a stock deal, the section will state that the buyer is buying stock directly from the owners of the business.

Aggregate Purchase Price

The next section will set out the purchase price. "Purchase Price" can mean many different things. Do we mean the total amount of cash being paid to the seller? Do we mean the cash plus the liabilities that the buyer is willing to absorb? Do we mean the cash plus the value of any buyer stock that the buyer is using to pay for the seller's business?

Normally, the purchase price section will start by stating the total amount of value that the buyer is paying, both today and at future times. This is called the "aggregate purchase price".

As an example, if the buyer is going to pay $1,000,000 at the closing and then pay another $500,000 a year from now if the business generates $2,000,000 of revenue during the year after the closing, then the "aggregate purchase price" is $1,500,000.

How the Purchase Price Gets Paid and When

The next part of the purchase price section provides a breakdown of each payment to be made, laying out the timing and the form of payment.

As an example, the aggregate purchase price for a target company's assets could be:

- $1,000,000 payable in cash at the closing by a wire transfer;
- $500,000 held in an escrow for one year to serve as a reserve against claims against the seller during that year;
- $1,000,000 in the form of a promissory note given by the buyer to the seller, with payment being made on the note if the seller gets a key customer consent or the business does $X million in revenue in the 1-3 years after the closing.

Let's talk more about the ways that payments can be made.

Cash

When it comes to being paid in cash, on small deals a seller may be willing to accept a check, usually a cashier's check issued by a bank after the bank actually received funds from the buyer. This kind of check should be immediately credited to the seller's account as soon as it is cashed.

Larger deals have cash payments made by wire transfer. A wire transfer is initiated from a buyer's bank account and goes straight to the seller's bank account. Unlike a regular check, the amount is creditable to the seller's account when it arrives.

Wire transfers require planning and thought. Banks have a "wire cutoff time", past which the bank can't guarantee that a wire transfer will actually be posted on the seller's account the same day. If you wire funds to me at 9 a.m., I will probably get the funds today. If you wire funds to me at 3 p.m., the odds are near zero I will get it today.

International wires can be complicated and take even more time. A wire from a bank in Europe could take a day or two to actually arrive.

The parties will want to make sure everyone is clear on what the wire deadlines and processing times are before agreeing to close. The buyer will be worried about sending funds before all of the closing conditions have been met. The seller will be worried about announcing a closing to all of its customers and employees before the money actually arrives.

Escrows

On small stock deals, a seller might get paid all of the purchase price in cash at the closing. On asset deals and larger deals, it is more common for some of the purchase price to be paid later. The buyer likes deferring payment to see if promised revenue actually shows up and to make sure that if the seller's promises about the state of the business are false, that the buyer does not have to chase the seller to get its money back or "claw back" the money.

The deferred payment is called an "earnout payment" if the payment only gets made if something happens (a "contingency") in the future. If the buyer has to pay $100 in six months, that's a "deferred payment." If a buyer has to pay $100 in six months, but only if the purchased business makes $5 in revenue during the six month period, then that's an earnout.

From the seller's perspective, if a payment is going to be deferred, the seller would prefer that the money for the deferred payment sit with a third party until it is time for the payment to be made. That way, the buyer can't "forget" or change its mind easily. When money sits with a third party, the money is said to be placed into "escrow."

When money goes into escrow, the buyer and seller will select a mutually agreeable party to serve as the "escrow agent". Escrow agents are usually companies that specialize in handling escrows. Lawyers, accountants and other service providers will typically be allergic to serving as an escrow agent because of the potential liability to both parties.

The escrow agent will hold the funds in escrow for a fee, with agreement on which party pays the fee being negotiable. The funds will stay in the escrow until a specific date passes or both parties send in written notices to the escrow agent confirming it's now ok to release the funds. If notices are required, the escrow agent will not release funds to any of the parties until the notices are received, period. The escrow agent does not want to be in the middle of a food fight between the buyer and seller, so it will just sit on the funds until the parties finally agree on the release terms or the escrow agent will deliver the escrowed funds to a court and let the parties fight it out in the courtroom.

Many non-lawyers are surprised and dismayed at the terms in the typical escrow agreement. The escrow agent wants to be thoroughly protected from angry buyers and sellers and will require both parties to agree, at length, that the escrow agent cannot be sued by anyone in the transaction unless the escrow agent either stole the money or did something incredibly stupid that would rise to the level of gross negligence (i.e. wired the money to a completely unrelated party). Deal lawyers understand that most of the escrow agreement templates are normal under market standards and will only lightly negotiate the terms unless the template has an egregious drafting bust.

Buyers will resist escrows. The buyer will have the funds put into escrow just sitting there instead of being available for use in the buyer's business. Buyers will view this as an "opportunity cost" – the money is unavailable. The buyer may want the seller to pay for the escrow agent's fees on the theory that the seller is getting the benefit of the security of the escrow mechanism, so it should pay for the cost.

Buyers will offer an escrow if the target company is being offered to multiple legitimate buyers or the deal can't get done without using one.

Promissory Notes

If a seller cannot get an escrow to cover a deferred payment, the seller may request that the deferred payment be covered in the form of a promissory note.

In its simplest form, a promissory note is a fancy form of IOU. The promissory note turns the promise to make the deferred payment into debt. The seller likes this because if a buyer ends up being unable to pay its bills and has to liquidate, the buyer's assets have to be used to pay off debts before any assets can be distributed to the buyer's equity holders.

Since promissory notes are commercial instruments like a check, only the buyer signs the note since the buyer is the only party with obligations under the terms of the note. The seller does not have to execute the note.

There are two types of debt that a seller should understand.

There are unsecured debts, where I owe you $100 but if I don't pay you, you can't claim direct ownership of my assets.

There are also secured debts, where Bank of America lends you $1,000,000, but they will only lend it to you if they can get a "secured interest" in all of the assets of your company. The bank puts a lien on your assets, telling the public that if your company liquidates, the bank gets first priority on grabbing and selling your assets to satisfy what you owe the bank. Anything left over goes to the unsecured creditors, and then finally to your shareholders.

If a seller has to take a promissory note, obviously the seller would prefer to get a secured promissory note to raise the odds that the seller actually collects the deferred payments. For deals where the buyer is small or doesn't rely on debt financing, the secured promissory note is a possibility.

However, life doesn't always work that way.

I have clients that have borrowed $200,000,000 to finance their businesses. The lenders are not remotely interested in allowing anyone to have a better place in line to grab my clients' assets, to put it mildly. If one of these clients offered to buy your business for $1,000,000, the client would not even ask its lenders if your promissory note could get higher priority because the lenders would laugh them off the phone.

That being said, getting an unsecured promissory note that puts the seller ahead of the equity holders is not a bad result in a situation like this.

A promissory note may have a "setoff" provision that makes the note less attractive. Here, the buyer has the right to reduce or skip a payment if the buyer has a claim for damages against the seller for something like a breach of a representation in the definitive agreement.

The Holdback -- Contract Right to a Future Payment

A seller's least favored form for a deferred payment is the holdback. In simple terms, the buyer agrees in the purchase agreement to make the deferred payment – the buyer "holds back" part of the purchase price. If the buyer doesn't pay, the seller can ask a court to enforce the contract.

This mechanism is used in deals where the deferred payment trigger is really simple ($1,000,000 will be paid on August 31, 20XX and there are no other conditions) or where the amount of the deferred payment is small enough that drafting a promissory note and dealing with collecting it for cancellation later is not worth the hassle.

The Buyer Uses a Shell Company to Make Deferred Payments

Larger buyers may have multiple entities that they use to run their businesses.

If a seller agrees to get some of the purchase price in the form of deferred payments or earnouts, the seller will want to make sure that any subsidiary used by the buyer to buy the target company will actually be substantial enough to still be around to make the future payments.

In situations like this, it may be reasonable for a seller to ask for a balance sheet for the buyer's subsidiary to show that the buyer has the cash or assets to be able to cover future payments. If the buyer subsidiary is thinly capitalized, the seller might ask the subsidiary's parent to guarantee future payments. Large public company buyers may be prohibited by their lenders from making guarantees for their subsidiaries; in situations like this, the seller will want to have one of their advisors review the buyer's public filings to confirm the buyer is healthy enough to cover the subsidiary's obligations to the seller or insist that the public company buyer get a waiver from its lenders.

Set-Offs; Elections; Purchase Price Allocations

The purchase and sale section will also contain a few other specialized clauses.

If there are deferred payments to be made, the buyer may ask for the right to reduce or cancel deferred payments if the buyer suffers losses from breaches of the seller's representations. The buyer's logic is that if the seller had undisclosed litigation that caused the buyer to suffer $100,000 in losses, it doesn't make any sense to pay the seller $100,000 only to have the seller send it right back to the buyer. Of course, the seller's fear is the buyer makes tenuous claims as an excuse to avoid paying what the buyer promised to pay at the start.

If the parties have agreed to have the buyer purchase the selling owner's stock, the section could contain the Section 336(e) or 338(h)(10) election language discussed in Chapter 9.

Another likely clause that may appear in this section would be a provision laying out how the purchase price will be allocated across the target company's assets. The purchase price allocation is helpful to assure that the buyer and seller don't report different allocations and cause each other problems when they report the transaction on their respective tax returns.

Closing Mechanics and Termination

The next section is a little schizophrenic.

This section sets out the anticipated date for the closing. While a specific date may be inserted, the closing date is usually qualified with language like "or such other date, time or place as the parties shall mutually agree". In simple terms, any specific date is purely aspirational and inserted to give the business folks a sense that the deal may actually close one day.

Next, the section will cover each of the documents that should be delivered when the closing is ready to occur. Here, the reader will find documents we mentioned earlier like escrow agreements and promissory notes. The list will also include certificates, employment agreements and a variety of other documents we will explore in greater detail in the next chapter.

The schizophrenia mentioned above appears in the clause covering termination. Not every deal that reaches the purchase agreement phase ends with a closing. If the buyer requires license transfers or contract consents that the seller simply can't deliver, the buyer may want the right to walk away from the deal. Similarly, if the deal takes a long time to close and the buyer gets into financial difficulty, the seller might want to walk away rather than fight to get deferred payments in a bankruptcy court. Consequently, any good purchase agreement will contain termination provisions. The provisions will normally include a "drop dead date", where either party can terminate if the closing hasn't happened by a particular date. In large deals, the seller may ask the buyer to pay a termination fee for "wasting" the seller's time and damaging its business if the deal doesn't actually close. As you can imagine, termination fees or "breakup fees" can be controversial during negotiations.

Seller's Representations and Warranties

In a large transaction, the section covering the seller's representations and warranties usually runs several pages. The seller's lawyer will typically review the representations on a clause by clause basis with the seller.

The buyer wants to make sure that the buyer fully understands the business being purchased. Consequently, the buyer will want the seller to describe basic facts about the target business in the actual purchase agreement. The buyer will also want to be able to go back to the seller and reclaim part of the purchase price if the seller failed to tell the buyer about problems with the business. If the seller makes a statement that is not accurate the seller is said to have "breached" the representation.

Lastly, if the closing is going to happen some time after the purchase agreement is signed – perhaps we need 60 days to get customers to agree to transfer the contracts from the seller to the buyer – then the buyer wants to make sure the buyer is not obligated to close if a major representation is no longer true. As an example, if the target company had no litigation when the purchase agreement was signed, but during the period between signing and closing the target company gets hit with a multi-million dollar lawsuit, the buyer may not want to buy the business . . . and the new litigation.

Here are a couple of examples of what representations look like:

"The Company is a corporation and is duly formed, validly existing and in good standing under the laws of the State of Oregon."

"The Company owns no real property."

"There is no claim pending or, to the Owner's knowledge, threatened against the Company."

Some sellers find the need for representations in the purchase agreement to be confusing. Why do I need to make pages of statements about the business when the buyer spent weeks looking at every document I had to provide during the due diligence phase?

The answer to this is simple: if the seller would like the buyer's money, the buyer has to be completely comfortable that the buyer isn't buying a damaged business. As Ronald Reagan used to say about weapons treaties with the Soviets, "trust but verify".

Representation Categories

Most purchase agreements will require representations covering these basic categories:

- Organization (Does the target company exist?)
- Subsidiaries
- Title to shares in a stock deal
- Title to assets in an asset deal
- No violation of corporate documents or contracts
- Financial statements
- Employee matters / benefit plans & ERISA

- Litigation
- Real property (owned property or leased property)
- Status of contracts
- Tax (did the company file its taxes? Still owe taxes? Any pending audits?)
- Compliance with laws / permits and licenses
- Intellectual property
- Environmental
- Relationships with related parties (any contracts between the target company and the owners or the owners' relatives?)
- Insurance
- Inventory
- Seller's obligations to pay brokers / investment bankers / finders because of the deal

The list will be longer if the target company operates in a regulated business like healthcare or banking. The purchase agreement may also include a representation that the purchase agreement and the disclosure schedules don't contain any untrue statements or omit (fail to include) material facts.

Disclosure Schedule

One of the biggest hold-ups in a deal is the preparation of the disclosure schedule. Lawyers can help a seller put the schedule together, but the seller and the target company management have to do the majority of the work organizing and confirming schedules. As an owner, you absolutely need to focus on helping put together the schedules and need to run the schedule creation parallel with the negotiation of the documents. Schedules can take weeks to put together, so waiting until after the documents are fully negotiated to start on drafting them will cause massive delays.

What is the disclosure schedule?

The representations will normally be drafted very broadly in the initial draft of the purchase agreement. For example, the initial draft may ask the seller to state that there is no litigation.

What if there _is_ litigation?

When there are facts that need to be disclosed to make a representation true, the facts are stated in a document that gets attached to the purchase agreement called a "disclosure schedule".

The disclosure schedule is usually broken out into sections, with the numbers matching the number of the section in the purchase agreement where the given representation appears. For example, if the representation on litigation is Section 3.6 in the purchase agreement, any litigation that needs to be disclosed will be listed in Section 3.6 of the disclosure schedule.

The representation itself will be modified in the next draft of the purchase agreement to now state: "**_Except as set forth in Section 3.6 of the disclosure schedule_**, there are no claims against the Company." This way, when we marry the representation to the disclosure schedule, the seller has accurately described the state of litigation at the target company.

The disclosure schedule will also contain lists.

As an example, the contracts representation may ask the seller to list all customer agreements that are currently in force. The disclosure schedule will include a section where the contracts are listed.

Listing every contract may get ridiculously long, so many times the buyer and seller will agree on a threshold for what is a "material contract" – perhaps the buyer really only cares about customer contracts where the annual revenue for the customer is $10,000 or more.

Unsophisticated sellers will sometimes want to just attach entire copies of the contracts to the disclosure schedule, either because they don't want to type up the list or they want to make sure the buyer can't "bite" the seller for something inside the contracts.

Sophisticated buyers will never accept attached contracts. Period. The buyer wants the seller to tell the buyer about any problems in the contracts via a disclosure in the schedules, not play a game of "gotcha" where the seller knew a bomb was lurking on page 23 of a contract.

The seller may wish to modify the representations with "qualifiers".

As discussed above, the contracts representation may be modified to only list contracts above a specific dollar threshold in value.

We discussed the "knowledge" qualifier in the definition section above. Before a seller goes bananas and qualifies every statement with a knowledge qualifier, it is important to understand the impact on the deal by using the qualifier.

If a seller states that there is no litigation, and there actually is litigation, then the liability attached to the litigation stays with the seller.

If a seller states that there is no litigation to its knowledge, and there is actually litigation that the seller doesn't know about, the buyer ends up with the liability.

The shifting back and forth of the liability is called "risk allocation".

The question for the buyer and the seller is who should bear the burden of the risk. If the seller should in all fairness know if it is named in a lawsuit, then the knowledge qualifier is unfair and the buyer will vigorously fight its use. If the seller faced the threat of a lawsuit but didn't have any way of knowing that a lawsuit was coming, then the knowledge qualifier might be fair.

The twin sister of the "knowledge" qualifier is the term "material". If the seller has a factory, the seller may be constantly in breach of minor OSHA regulations, like every other company in the seller's industry. The buyer may be willing to let the seller qualify its representation that the target company is not in "material" breach of OSHA regulations.

However, the use of materiality qualifiers is also a risk allocation mechanism and should be used judiciously in the seller's markup to avoid stalled negotiations with the buyer, unless the seller has serious leverage.

Buyer's Representations and Warranties

The buyer will also make representations in the purchase agreement.

If the buyer is paying the purchase price using only cash, the buyer may only offer representations that the buyer exists, has the cash to do the deal, is not prohibited by its own corporate documents or contracts from doing the deal, is authorized by its board or shareholders to do the deal and hasn't hired any brokers or other parties that may look to the seller for their fees.

If the buyer is using the buyer's stock or other securities to buy the target business, the buyer's representations could end up looking a lot like the seller's representations, since the seller is now effectively an investor in the buyer's company once it takes some of the buyer's equity.

Pre-Closing Covenants

If the transaction requires time after the purchase agreement is signed to obtain contract assignment consents or regulatory approval, then the purchase agreement may also include covenants regarding the conduct of the parties during the time between signing and closing.

A "positive" covenant is a binding promise to take an action. Examples include promises by the seller to encourage employees to stay and for the seller to use its commercially reasonable efforts to actually go out and obtain all necessary contract consents.

A "negative" covenant is a binding promise <u>not</u> to take an action. An example is a covenant by the seller not to do anything "outside the ordinary course of business," like giving employees of the target company a big raise between signing and closing or selling off assets that are part of the deal.

Post-Closing Covenants

The purchase agreement will also include covenants about the conduct of the parties after the closing has occurred.

The buyer may require the seller to agree to a non-compete provision. The buyer does not want the seller to set up a new shop conducting the same business in a nearby location the day after the closing. Usually the provision sets out a clear time period when the covenant will govern and sets geographic boundaries and a description of what "competing" means.

The parties will also have covenants binding each party to coordinate with the others when reporting the transaction in their respective tax returns.

Closing Conditions

The next section will cover closing conditions. If the transaction is simple and can close without third party consents or license transfers, then there may be no need for closing conditions.

If there will be a signing of the purchase agreement followed by a delayed closing, then the parties will want to lay out what has to happen before they are each obligated to follow through with closing the transaction.

At a minimum, the closing conditions will include a requirement that there be no litigation aimed at stopping the deal, that all necessary consents and approvals have been obtained, and that the various additional documents required to do the deal have been actually fully executed.

The closing conditions will include a requirement that the seller obtain all consents from third parties required to transfer contracts from the seller to the buyer.

The closing conditions may also require the approval of the board of directors or shareholders of the buyer or the seller, or both.

There may also be a requirement that the buyer have completed its due diligence investigation to its satisfaction. This can be a reasonable condition if the buyer negotiated the purchase agreement at the same time it started diligence and hasn't had time to fully complete its work.

Lastly, the buyer may require that there have been no material adverse change to the target business before the closing.

These last three closing conditions allow the buyer an "out" to avoid closing and should draw close scrutiny by the seller. The seller wants to make sure that the buyer is obligated to follow through on closing, while the buyer wants to create flexibility for itself if the deal looks less attractive after time has passed.

Indemnification

The indemnification section is normally the hardest section to read and understand, even for lawyers.

At its most basic, the section states that if a party gets stuck with a liability or loss that it didn't agree to accept, that the other party will handle the liability or loss. Usually, it's the seller indemnifying the buyer, but the buyer could theoretically harm the seller too, so the section is usually drafted to be somewhat reciprocal.

Survival Period

The section will typically start by covering how long a harmed party has to discover and make a claim against the other party based on a breach of the other party's representations. The period is called the "survival period".

The survival period will come in three flavors.

First, there are some representations that are so fundamental that they should in theory last forever. As an example, if the buyer purchases the sellers assets and it turns out that the seller didn't actually own the assets, then the buyer should be able to get its money back whenever it finally figures out the problem. The buyer's perspective is if the seller is worried about this kind of issue surfacing ten or twenty years later, it shouldn't sell its assets. The list of fundamental representations is usually very short.

Second, there are representations that cover areas where the laws allow someone to pursue a claim related to the topic for a limited period of time. As an example, representations regarding tax matters are usually limited to the period of time during which a tax authority could chase the target company – i.e. six or seven years. The period is called a "statute of limitations".

Third, there are representations that are important to the buyer and but aren't critical. For example, the buyer wants to know that relationships between the target company and its employees are good. There is no statute of limitations covering this topic, so the parties will agree to a specific period. The buyer may want the period to last for 24 to 36 months, while the seller will argue for 12 months on the theory that one year ought to be plenty of time to figure out whether the seller missed a disclosure on the issue. The period for this category is frequently negotiated.

Categories of Claims

Next, the section will cover the type of breaches for which indemnification should be provided. In addition to breaches of representations, the parties will want to be covered for losses caused by the other party's breach of covenants, failure to pay its taxes or losses that come from liabilities that the buyer specifically excluded from the deal. The parties will also want specific coverage of liabilities coming from fees owed to a broker or finder, even though the topic is specifically covered by a representation.

The section will then turn to the procedure for how to handle a claim by a third party related to a breached representation. For example, if the buyer is sued by a customer of the target company for a product failure that happened on the seller's watch, the buyer would want to hand the claim to the seller and have the seller deal with it. The procedures are usually highly technical and detailed.

Cap on Liability

A critical section for any seller is the provision covering the cap on the liability for each party for indemnifiable losses.

The buyer would like to know that if losses from the target company that came out of breached representations actually add up to the purchase price, that the buyer can get its money back. If the target business is in a dangerous industry (i.e., asbestos, nuclear power), the buyer may want a cap on the seller's liability that goes far in excess of the purchase price.

The seller will be motivated to use the purchase price as the very highest number it might agree to for the cap on its liability. If the seller has multiple potential buyers, the seller may be able to convince the bidders to agree to a percentage of the purchase price and assume the risk that claims could go above the specific percentage.

There are usually exceptions to the cap as well. If the seller committed fraud or an intentional breach, then the cap may be drafted to not apply in that situation.

Baskets and Deductibles

The seller will be concerned that a buyer may come after the seller for very small claims, or a death by a thousand cuts.

One way to alleviate this concern is for the seller to request a "basket" or "deductible."

A "basket" is a mechanism where the buyer can hand minor claims to the seller, but only after the minor (and major) claims add up to a specific dollar amount. For example, if the parties agree that $50,000 is a reasonable number for the seller to cover, the seller won't have to cover claims until the basket is "full" – the total claims equal or exceed $50,000. In a true "basket", once the claims hit the dollar threshold the basket "tips over" and the seller has to cover all of the claims, from the first dollar onward.

With a "deductible", the parties agree that anything below a specific dollar amount is just immaterial. In this case, the seller doesn't have to cover any losses below the immaterial amount. As an example, if the purchase price is $1,000,000, the parties may agree that the buyer won't bother the seller with claims adding up to $30,000. However, any claims above and beyond $30,000 have to be covered by the seller.

The amounts of a basket or deductible are always negotiable, and a buyer in a strong position may not agree to a basket or deductible at all.

"Miscellaneous" Section

The most unloved section of the purchase agreement is the "miscellaneous" section. Most folks refer to it as "boilerplate". I refer to it as other people's life lessons.

While clauses with titles like "entire agreement" and "severability" are ones that a seller will want to leave to the seller's lawyers, there are a few provisions worth highlighting in this section.

Sometimes lawyers will intentionally, or just out of habit, insert an attorney's fees clause. This clause requires the loser in a dispute over the interpretation of the contract to pay the winner's legal fees. This sounds great, until you imagine yourself as the potential loser. Some lawyers like the clause, I'm not a fan based on the unpredictability of how the scenario will ultimately play out.

The section may also contain a dispute resolution section. In states like California, the courts have severe backlogs of cases. Consequently, a contract dispute can take years to get to trial. Having a clause in the purchase agreement that requires the parties to go to arbitration can accelerate the ability of the parties to get their dispute resolved if it actually goes all the way to arbitration. These clauses also have "loser pays the winner's attorneys' fees" language and has to be read carefully.

Infrequently, the miscellaneous section may actually contain clauses that are anything but "boilerplate". Sometimes parties will stick requirements that a parent guarantee its buyer subsidiary's obligations here or put in language allowing a third party to make claims under the purchase agreement. The seller's lawyers should scrub the section to catch material clauses like these examples.

Signature Pages

Normally the signature pages to a purchase agreement are uncontroversial.

However, the seller should look at the signature page to make sure that the seller understands exactly who all of the parties are to the deal to avoid surprises.

The signature pages will also sometimes hint at who the true decision makers are in the deal. If the seller is negotiating with the buyer's VP of mergers and acquisitions, but the buyer's signing officer is actually the chief financial officer, you can guess who actually gets to make the decision on whether to do the deal.

Exhibits

Many people get confused over the difference between exhibits and schedules, including lawyers.

I was told many moons ago that an exhibit is a form of document that will be executed at the closing. A promissory note would be a good example.

A schedule is a document containing information that you need to understand the purchase agreement. A list of the seller's customer agreements would be a schedule, not an exhibit.

In theory, the key documents to be signed later in a deal should be attached as exhibits. This works great if the documents have been drafted and agreed on at the time the purchase agreement is signed. If the parties are in a hurry to sign the purchase agreement, the exhibits may consist of pages with exhibit headings and the words "to come" instead of actual documents.

To the extent that the seller can stay disciplined and require that the exhibits – at least the key ones – be drafted and settled on before signing the purchase agreement, the lower the odds are that the seller will be surprised before the closing with secondary documents containing new terms or very different interpretations of how the secondary documents should work.

Schedules

While the disclosure schedules have been discussed at length above, it is worth adding a final note on them regarding how the disclosures actually work.

Section 3.9 covered whether the seller was in compliance with its material contracts. Imagine the seller discloses in Section 3.9 of the disclosure schedule that Chevron is a customer of the target company and is unhappy about the way a specific service was provided.

The question for the parties would be whether the disclosure about Chevron in Section 3.9 of the schedules had to be made again in Section 3.3 of the schedules, covering potential litigation.

The seller could address this a couple ways. First, it could include a cover page to the schedules, stating that a disclosure in one section of the schedules is intended to be disclosure in any other section where the specific disclosure would be obvious or "reasonably apparent". Alternatively, the seller could just include a statement like "See Schedule 3.9, Item 5 (Chevron)" in the litigation schedule.

The seller should note that there may be other schedules in addition to the disclosure schedule. If there are multiple selling shareholders in a stock sale, the purchase agreement may have a schedule listing the wire instructions for each selling stockholder's bank account so the buyer knows where to send each selling stockholder's part of the purchase price.

Conclusion

By working through this chapter, you have now learned how the purchase agreement is constructed. You know the key provisions that you will want to personally review and why the provisions are important to you as the business person and not just to your lawyers.

Chapter 11: The Secondary Documents

What We Will Learn

While the purchase agreement provides the structure for the transaction, the secondary documents are each important in their own way and worth understanding as a seller. This chapter will review documents that are most likely to appear in a sale transaction.

As a preliminary note in case the reader skipped Chapter 10, escrow agreements and promissory notes are discussed in great detail in the previous chapter.

Employment and Consulting Agreements

Employees are valuable assets in most target companies. The employees with the most knowledge may prove to be key to a buyer. Consequently, the buyer will want to make sure that the target's institutional memory doesn't walk out the door, at least not until the buyer is able to absorb most of such knowledge.

The primary tools for retaining key employees are the employment agreement and the consulting agreement.

If buyer wants to retain a key management team member, the buyer may offer to enter into an employment agreement with the manager.

The typical employment agreement will cover the following topics:

- Title
- Reporting responsibility

- Salary, bonus, vacation and benefits
- Circumstances when termination may occur
- Severance owed on termination
- How the company's trade secrets and other intellectual property are handled on the employee's departure
- Possible non-competition clause / non-solicitation provisions

The first three items can be easily covered in a simple offer letter.

The employee likes the employment agreement because the employee can get guaranteed severance if the company decides to terminate the employee.

In employer friendly states, the employer gets a major benefit for agreeing to do an employment agreement, in the form of a non-competition provision. The employer can require the employee to agree to not create a competing business or work for one during a period of time after the employee leaves the company's employment. In states like California that are employee friendly, a non-competition clause is only valid if it's given by a person in connection with the sale of that person's business, not if it's given by an employee solely in connection with that person's employment.

However, in some states the employer can benefit from an employment agreement by requiring an employee to comply with a non-solicitation clause. The clause requires the employee to agree not to solicit the company's employees or customers after the employee leaves the company. The clause can also require the employee to agree not to interfere with the company's relationships with the company's vendors.

The buyer in a deal may offer to give employment agreements to a manager as a way to give an extra incentive to stay after the deal closes and confirm for the manager that the manager really does have a future post-closing with the buyer's team. Consequently how severance would work and what would trigger severance become important, with extra emphasis needing to be placed on what type of termination would be an appropriate trigger.

"Termination" can mean different things depending on the circumstances.

"Termination for cause" usually means the company terminated the employee for doing something truly awful – committing fraud, insubordination, willful misconduct. Most employment agreements have carefully tailored lists of actions that fall inside the definition of "cause". As you can imagine, severance usually isn't given if termination is for cause. That being said, an employee that is terminated for cause may very well want to litigate over whether there was actually cause.

"Termination without cause" means that the company terminated the employee without the employee doing anything to provoke the termination. The employee may be terminated because the employee's position is no longer necessary or just because the employer wants to go in a different direction. Termination without cause is a typical trigger for owing severance.

"Constructive termination" is another category that can trigger severance. Here, the employee is not formally terminated, but the employee's terms of employment get a radical adjustment. Instead of being chief financial officer reporting to the president in Los Angeles for $200K base salary, the CFO wakes up one day as the chief janitorial officer reporting to the receptionist from his new office in Alaska with a zero missing on his base salary. The employee is still employed, but his whole world changed – he has been "constructively" terminated.

Most buyers will offer employment agreements only to critical employees, rather than folks that can be easily replaced. Severance offered on a grand scale can make an acquisition disastrous in the long run.

Consulting agreements are used in a similar situation, where the buyer would like a key manager to stay for a specific period of time that allows the buyer to do a "brain drain" on the manager. If a business owner is selling her business in order to retire, the buyer may ask the owner to stay on as a consultant for a few months to help introduce the buyer to key customers, walk the buyer through how the finances were being managed and to assist with onboarding the target company's employees into the buyer's organization. Once a few months have passed and the buyer feels confident that it understands the acquired business, the owner is then free to retire.

Transition Services Agreements

If the seller is only selling a piece of its business, like a division or a product line, the part being sold may not be self-sustaining on the first day after the closing. In situations where a division contains only engineers and not HR, finance and sales personnel, the buyer may need the target company to continue serving as the "mother ship" for a few months to keep the division functioning while the buyer starts hooking the engineering employees and the division's customers and vendors into its own systems.

The parties will enter into a transition services agreement to cover this scenario. The seller will provide carefully described services to the buyer or the new entity holding the division after the closing. Usually, the buyer will pay for the transition services at a cost equal to what it costs the seller to provide the services, or perhaps on a "cost plus" basis where the seller gets a slight percentage increase on its costs to compensate it for the administrative hassle of helping the offloaded division – and to encourage the buyer not to take advantage of the transition services beyond a time frame that is absolutely necessary.

Bills of Sale, Termination Statements and Assignments

In an asset deal, most states have a set of statutes called a "commercial code." The code requires that, even though there is an asset purchase agreement, there be a separate document documenting the transfer of the seller's assets to the buyer. The bill of sale, like a promissory note, is a commercial document and is typically only signed by the seller.

When assets are being sold, the buyer will run a "UCC search". The buyer checks with the state and the county where the assets are located to see if any third parties have put a claim or "lien" on the assets under the Uniform Commercial Code, or "UCC". If there are liens on the assets by a bank that lent money to the seller or a vendor of the seller, then the buyer will require that the seller pay off the loan or vendor (either before the closing or with the buyer sending part of the purchase price at the closing to the bank or vendor instead of to the seller). When the lien is paid, the buyer will want a "termination statement" filed with the state or county to make the record of the lien go away. Then the buyer can be certain that it owns the assets without any third party claiming otherwise.

The sister to the bill of sale is an "assignment and assumption agreement." In simple terms, this document helps transfer the rights and obligations of the seller under the seller's contracts with its customers and vendors to the buyer.

There may also be a third document called an "intellectual property assignment agreement." This document will set out how the seller's intellectual property is transferred to the buyer.

119

Certificates

As discussed a few times in other chapters, not every deal closes when the purchase agreement is signed. If there are consents or license transfers that need to happen between the time the purchase agreement is signed and the closing actually happens, then there is a possibility that facts about each party may have changed by the time the closing rolls around.

Consequently, the buyer will want a "bring down" certificate from the seller. The seller is asked to have an officer certify that there have been no material changes to the target business or any of the representations made about it in the purchase agreement. The certificate is signed as of the date of the closing. The certificate is called a "bring down" certificate because the representations made when the purchase agreement was signed (i.e., July) are now "brought down" and confirmed as still true as of the closing (i.e., December). The certificate will also have the seller confirm that the seller complied with all of its covenants during the period between signing and closing.

The buyer will also want to know that the seller's constituents have all agreed to do the deal. The seller will have an officer sign a second certificate called an "incumbency" certificate. This certificate confirms that the person signing the documents for the seller really has the authority to do so. The certificate also confirms that resolutions have been approved by the seller's board of directors (and possibly the seller's shareholders) that allow the deal to go through. Lastly, the certificate will attach the seller's governing documents (articles, bylaws, etc.) so the buyer can look at them to confirm the resolutions were enough to approve the deal. While the buyer may have seen the governing documents during due diligence, the buyer wants the seller to certify that the buyer actually looked at the right versions.

The buyer will also want "good standing" certificates. The good standing certificate is issued by the state where the target company is incorporated. This certificate confirms that the target company actually exists and is "in good standing" – meaning that the company is allowed to actually do business and hasn't had its existence suspended for failure to pay taxes or other reasons. In many states, the Secretary of State's office will issue the good standing certificate; in a state like California the state tax authority will also issue one.

Opinion Letters

In complex deals, a buyer may require that the seller's lawyers give a written opinion about specific issues about the seller's structure or business. The opinion is issued in the form of a letter addressed by the seller's lawyers to the buyer.

If the target company's books are messy, the buyer may want the seller's lawyers to confirm that the selling shareholders in a stock sale actually own all of their shares and the shares they own actually add up to 100% of the shares.

If there are important tax features to the deal, the parties may want an opinion on the tax structure from tax lawyers.

Law firms don't like issuing opinion letters. By issuing a letter to the buyer, the law firm is essentially agreeing that the buyer can rely on it. Reliance means the buyer can sue the seller's lawyers if the opinion doesn't hold up. Effectively, the buyer is asking the law firm to be really, really sure that an important legal conclusion is correct, and to specify the law firm's level of certainty about the given conclusion.

The buyer likes this result if the seller's law firm is large because the law firm may have deeper pockets than the sellers themselves. Asking for a small law firm or solo lawyer to give an opinion doesn't provide a similar benefit and most buyers won't ask a small firm to issue one.

Since law firms are worried about the liability of giving an opinion, they will typically charge a premium for issuing the letter. For the seller, this means additional legal costs.

The opinion letter itself will usually run several pages. The first few pages will list a number of assumptions made about the matter at hand. Then another few pages will list all of the qualifications and exceptions that should be read into the opinion being given. Finally, the letter will state the actual opinion itself. It's quite a series of gyrations.

Flow of Funds

Complicated deals with multiple payments being made to multiple sellers at different times with different bank accounts will use a "flow of funds" document to help the accounting teams at both the buyer and seller keep track of incoming and outgoing payments.

The document can be prepared by either party or their lawyers and is usually not signed by the parties.

Conclusion

There may be other documents that are required for a specific transaction, but the documents described above are the most typical. Understanding the extra moving pieces beyond just the purchase agreement can help sellers get comfortable with the blizzard of paper that comes as a deal gets closer to the closing. We now also understand the key elements of these different documents and can see where the seller will need to make business decisions on how they are structured.

Chapter 12: What Happens between Signing and Closing

What We Will Learn

We have mentioned that deals will sometimes have a period between the signing of a purchase agreement and the actual closing. The period allows the seller to obtain consents for the assignment of its contracts to the buyer. The period also allows for time to get regulatory approvals and license transfers completed. This chapter will explore the pre-closing period in greater detail to let sellers know what to expect and how to plan so the period can be as short as reasonably possible.

Customers, Vendors and the Landlord

During the pre-closing period, the buyer will be keenly interested in finding out how solid the relationship is between the target company and its customers.

Sellers are reluctant to let a buyer talk to customers for obvious reasons. The seller doesn't want to scare its customers and give them an excuse to start looking for a more "stable" vendor. The seller also worries that the buyer may try to steal customers if the sale transaction doesn't work out.

Consequently, the seller may want to avoid allowing the buyer to do customer calls during the due diligence period that occurs before the purchase agreement is signed. Once the agreement is executed, in theory the risk of losing the deal goes down for the seller, and most sellers will allow for joint customer calls, where the seller and the buyer both approach key customers to explain the deal and why the customers should be comfortable with the buyer taking over the target company's business.

The customer calls go hand in hand with seeking contract assignment consents. As discussed in prior chapters, the seller's contracts may contain assignment provisions that require the other party's prior written consent before a new party can take over the seller's rights and obligations. In these situations, the seller will want to call the party with the consent right, explain the deal and then send a letter requesting consent by a counter-signature by the other party.

If the seller has a strong relationship with the other party and the other party is fairly small, the consent process can be short. If the other party is a Fortune 500 company, the other party's lawyers may need to review the consent . . . and the consent can take weeks to get attention.

Further, landlords frequently include language in their leases not only requiring consent, but also requiring the tenant (meaning the seller) to pay for the landlord's "expenses" in reviewing the consent request. Sometimes, the expenses are the landlord's bill from its law firm, sometimes it's a specific fee stated in the lease for a few thousand dollars.

The consent request could also result in the seller's worst fear: the other party decides to not grant consent and instead terminates the agreement.

Given the risks involved, the seller wants to make sure the seller has identified potential consent problems and delays before signing the purchase agreement. The organized seller also designates a person that will "bird-dog" the consent process and stay on top of each consent and its status so there are no surprises. Having a consent chart to track the status of each consent, with a meeting to review the status once every few days with the buyer's team can help avoid surprises and unnecessary tension.

Another area that the seller will want to be prepared for is handling contract extensions in cases where a key contract is about to expire or come up for renewal shortly before or after the closing. A smart buyer will look at a three year contract that is set to expire one month after the closing and ask the seller to get an extension as a requirement for closing. The seller may want to even get extensions before starting the selling process to avoid having to ask a customer or key vendor for an extension at the same time the seller is asking for a consent to assignment. Done too late in the process, the request for an extension can put the seller in a tough position, with the other party asking for concessions it may not have been able to get if the seller had not been in such a vulnerable position.

The seller should also anticipate that there are contracts that the buyer will not want. The buyer may not need the seller's facility. The buyer may already have contracts with the seller's customer or vendor, with better terms. In these situations, the seller may have to either retain the contract if the sale is an asset deal or terminate the contract.

Employee Issues: Communications, Meetings and Layoffs

Managing communications with employees during a sale process brings a wide variety of concerns for the seller. The seller may want to avoid giving employees a long runway to search for other employment. Sellers also worry that if a transaction fails, the employees will be demoralized and leave even if the company is in decent shape. Sellers will fear that an unethical buyer may find out that there are really only three key employees out of the fifty employees working at the target company, and just steal the three key people and drop the transaction.

During most diligence processes, the buyer will have spoken with key employees before the purchase agreement is signed, if only because the key employees are the ones that are capable of explaining the target company's financials, research and development efforts and sales strategy.

The buyer will want to talk to the rest of the target's employees prior to closing the deal to see how the other employees will fit into the buyer's culture and to see if the other employees are competent and necessary. The seller may want to sit in on interviews to make sure the buyer doesn't damage relationships. The seller and buyer will need to resolve tensions over the process in advance to make sure that the seller's concerns about relationship damage don't become a self-fulfilling prophecy.

The buyer will also want to give the seller an opportunity to volunteer folks that need to be terminated. The seller may have been carrying underperforming employees to avoid the unpleasantness of terminating people or scaring other employees with a larger layoff, and can now use the transaction as a reasonable excuse for thinning the workforce. The buyer has to be very careful not to let the process make the buyer look like a bad guy, since the seller may be leaving the picture while the buyer is trying to retain the bulk of the workforce.

The buyer's human resource team will need time to work with the target company to make sure that the seller's employees can be efficiently onboarded onto the buyer's payroll systems and benefit plans. Sometimes the buyer's team only finds out about the deal at the very end, and the process can be chaotic.

When the transaction is ready to close, normally the buyer and seller will send management representatives to the target company's facilities to announce the formal closing and welcome the employees being retained.

If more than a handful of target employees are going to be laid off as part of the transaction, the seller and the buyer will want to make sure their lawyers are thinking about potential regulatory issues. For large deals, there are federal laws, including the WARN Act, that require advance notice to employees where 50 or more employees are going to be laid off at any given facility. The WARN Act was geared toward preventing large companies like auto manufacturers from suddenly closing a car plant without any warning to the community.

Lastly, as a reminder for those readers that may have skipped Chapter 11 on secondary documents, the buyer may want or need to negotiate employment agreements with the target company's key employees during the pre-closing period. The key employees may retain their own lawyers to assist them in negotiating with the buyer, so the negotiations may not always go quickly. The parties also will need to focus on terminating the target company's incentive plans, stock option plans and other benefit plans and transitioning the target company's employees to the buyer's new plans.

Regulatory Approval, Licenses, Permits

For very large deals, the federal government worries about the impact that such a deal may have on competition in the marketplace. The Hart-Scott-Rodino Act allows the Department of Justice and the Federal Trade Commission to review deals to see if the combination of the buyer and the seller will concentrate so much market power in one set of hands that the country will be hurt. As an example, if the buyer has 60% of the business in computer monitors and the seller has 30% of the business in computer monitors, the two companies combined could raise prices or lower quality and consumers wouldn't be able to do very much about it, at least in the short term.

In a regulated industry, there may be agencies with oversight over the target company's business that may have to approve the deal. Banks and defense industry companies would want to think through the regulatory process specific to them.

On a similar note, businesses that require licenses to operate may take time to sell. In the restaurant industry, sometimes the license to serve alcohol is worth more than the business itself. Businesses that can only be owned and operated by licensed professionals also require planning on the license front, such as law firms, accounting practices and medical practices.

Databases and IT Systems

Buyers in information-intensive businesses, like health insurance companies or banks will expect to need time to migrate the target company's information on to the buyer's own servers. The seller should expect that during the pre-closing period, the seller's IT team will need to be available (and cooperative) as the buyer tries to map what the seller has and how to "port" the data across.

Similarly, if the seller's IT network is configured differently than what the buyer has or is running outdated equipment, the IT teams will need to coordinate and plan carefully for the post-closing integration. The sooner the teams are introduced to each other, the more likely the transaction will be successful.

Handling Retained Liabilities

If the seller has ongoing litigation, the seller should probably start planning during the pre-closing process about how the seller is going to manage the dispute. At a minimum, the seller will need to retain or have access to the business's records. The seller will also likely need to keep access to any employees that will be joining the buyer's work force.

If the seller is going to retain other liabilities (i.e., the buyer doesn't want to keep a facility and the seller has to keep the lease), the seller may want to negotiate during the pre-closing process with the parties on the other end of the liability to try to make the liability go away sooner rather than later to make post-closing life easier for the seller.

Conclusion

In this chapter, we have identified areas where the seller needs to be disciplined and work a process to keep the pre-closing process as short as possible. The seller is now aware that the seller will have to focus not only on contract assignments and employee relations, but also on less obvious areas like database integration and regulatory issues.

Chapter 13: The Pre-Closing

What We Will Learn

In this chapter, you will learn about:

- How your team will prepare for a successful closing
- Gating items that can cause the date for a closing to slip
- What to do when disaster strikes before the closing

Preparation

During a few decades of legal practice, I have worked on dozens of closings. The closings that went smoothly all had one thing in common: each of the parties stayed focused on the transaction from start to finish. The parties made time to organize documents, get signatures for closing documents in advance and had payment instructions ready and in the right hands before the main event.

The drama-filled closings almost always involved parties that timed their vacations for the day after the closing, on the assumption that the date would never slip. These closings had parties that did not want to sign until the last minute, causing frantic races to track down signatures or attempt to waive them in order to get a deal closed. The closings also had parties with unrealistic assumptions about how cooperative third parties would be when asked to sign things like consents with only a week to go before the closing. Sellers sometimes found themselves only getting part of the money they were supposed to be paid on the closing date because key parts of the transaction couldn't be finished until weeks or months later.

As a seller, your goal is to aim for the organized, stress-free closing. Let's talk about how to make that happen and avoid the horror stories above.

Knowing When You are Near the Finish Line

Parties that have successful closings understand that when parties agree in January to a closing date of March 31st, that the March 31st date is "aspirational". If the seller starts making financial commitments based on getting money for her business on March 31st, the seller could be embarrassed when March 31st comes and the deal is weeks away from closing.

The closing date for a deal becomes more real when the key "gating items" have been obtained.

Gating Items

A typical list of gating items would include:

- The purchase agreement is fully executed.

- The schedules are complete (sometimes the purchase agreement will be signed when the schedules are only partially complete, with some schedules just having placeholders like "to come").

- Customer, vendor and landlord consents have not only been requested but are actually signed and in hand.

- Regulatory approvals have been finalized and are in hand.

- If the buyer is paying with borrowed money, the loan has been approved and funds have actually been provided by the lender to the buyer.

- If shareholder approvals are required on either side, the necessary number of votes have been obtained to go forward with the deal.

- Getting wire instructions for each party that will be getting paid out of the money being paid by the buyer.

  o If the buyer is purchasing shares from the owners of the selling business, there may be multiple bank accounts that need to be listed.

  o If the seller has debt that needs to be paid at the closing, the buyer needs to know who the lenders are and what the information is to pay off the loans. Normally, the lender will provide a "payoff letter" as of a specific date and wire instructions. If the closing slips past the specific date, the seller may have to get a fresh payoff letter from the lender.

  o If payment is being made to more than one party, the parties should prepare a "flow of funds" memorandum, laying out exactly who is getting paid how much and when so all of the payments actually happen in a relatively stress-free manner.

The lawyers on each side should be trading a closing checklist back and forth that shows what documents are outstanding and who is responsible for obtaining them. However, the seller should also be keeping an eye on how the closing checklist is progressing, since a number of gating items will really be under the seller's control.

As discussed in the last chapter, the time it takes to obtain contract consents is inherently unpredictable because the power to give the consents is in the hands of third parties. This is where the seller needs to use the seller's relationships with the other parties to the seller's contracts to keep the process from being any longer than it has to be.

While the seller's lawyer can send requests for contract consents to the seller's landlord, the seller probably has the best chance of actually getting the consent signed since the seller probably knows the landlord personally. If the seller walks the consent to the landlord and hands it to the landlord's building manager, the odds of getting the consent signed – and signed quickly – go way up.

In Chapter 10, we noted that a buyer will require that all contract consents be obtained before the buyer is obligated to close the deal. If the seller has 100 contracts that require third party consent to transfer them, the seller may not be able to get all of the consents. What happens then?

Normally, a buyer will be most concerned customer contracts that represent that bulk of the seller's revenue, vendor contracts for goods or services that are hard to replace (at least at the price or timing that the seller is getting) and facility leases. If the seller cannot obtain a consent from the copy machine vendor or a customer that represents 0.0001% of the seller's revenue, the buyer may agree to "waive" the requirement to obtain that particular consent. However, the buyer will apply maximum pressure on the seller to get as many of the immaterial consents as well as the major ones until the last moment. Smart sellers will not slough off on obtaining consents to minor contracts.

On a similar note about shareholder approvals, the seller's lawyer can send out a shareholder consent for signature, but if the seller makes phone calls to the shareholders in advance and does follow up phone calls, the process of getting the consent fully executed improves dramatically.

A steady, relentless focus on gating items will make for a smooth closing.

The Pre-Closing

Experienced lawyers will frequently try to orchestrate a call with the buyer's lawyers a few days in advance of a scheduled closing – if we want to actually close on March 31st, holding a pre-closing call on March 29th is generally a good idea.

The pre-closing call will allow the parties to methodically go through each document. The parties will confirm that they each have the final version of the document. They will exchange signature pages during the pre-closing to make sure each side isn't missing any autographs. Usually the parties will qualify the signature exchange by telling the other party that their side's signature pages are being delivered to "be held in escrow" until they give permission to release, with the qualifier being given to avoid an accidentally pre-mature closing. I've never seen a pre-mature closing, but lawyers are risk adverse by nature, and usually include the escrow qualification as a matter of course.

The parties will also go through the consent checklist to make sure that all of the necessary consents are actually signed and in everyone's possession.

The parties will also confirm that the wire instructions have been given to the buyer's finance team and the wire transfers are ready to go when word is given that the closing is complete.

If wire transfers are coming from overseas, the parties will want to make sure that the foreign buyer wires money from the buyer's overseas bank account to a domestic bank account in advance of the closing. If this isn't watched carefully, funds could get "wired" on March 31st, but not actually arrive until the wire is routed from Moscow, to London, and finally to Los Angeles . . . on April 3rd. Ouch.

If anything is missing, the parties can negotiate over how they want to handle the missing items. If the copy machine contract consent is missing, the buyer may waive it. If key consents are missing, the buyer may insist on delaying the closing.

The obvious benefit of the pre-closing is to shake out action items that one party forgot or downplayed and fix problems before the closing itself.

How to Handle the Bumpy Pre-Closing

When I was a senior lawyer at one of the big law firms, I once had a junior lawyer come into my office in a panic. Our client was gearing up for a closing and we were missing a key signature. I congratulated the junior lawyer.

The lawyer looked perplexed. I told him that there are usually three "oh my gods" that happen before a deal is truly ready to close. The junior lawyer had just seen the first "oh my god" crisis. That meant two more were coming and the deal was actually going to happen.

Obviously, the preference is to have a smooth closing, as we just finished discussing in the first half of this chapter. However, life doesn't always go as planned, and maintaining one's cool under pressure is a valuable skill.

Most problems that come up during the pre-closing phase are going to be solvable. Usually pre-closing issues come in a couple of flavors.

First, the consent from the key customer not only doesn't arrive signed, but instead shows up with extortion requests – the contract transfer to the buyer is only acceptable if the term is reduced by one year and the price of the products being purchased is lowered by 25%. In situations like this, sometimes the buyer will be willing to buy the seller's business without the contract consent, as long as the seller agrees to keep the seller's company open and continue to administer the contract on behalf of the buyer. The buyer performs the work as a subcontractor for the seller, and the seller sends all payments from the customer to the buyer without any markdown.

The next possible scenario is a government agency's refusal to grant regulatory approval of a deal. This scenario usually surfaces in very large deals where the federal government is worried that the combination of two very large players in an industry would hurt the industry's customers by giving the newly combined company the ability to increase prices at will because of its new power to dominate the industry. Typically, the government agencies overseeing these situations – called antitrust approvals (or HSR approvals after the Hart-Scott-Rodino Act that governs antitrust issues) – will refuse to grant approval but will allow a possible solution. The government may decide that two large hotel companies can go ahead with their merger, as long as they sell off hotels in areas where they would control the market.

Another possible issue that comes up, usually at the last minute, is the key employee who suddenly refuses to sign an employment agreement with the buyer. This employee decides that they have enough leverage to ask for a higher salary, a signing bonus or other economic perk. Usually, the employee overestimates the employee's true importance to the business, but not always. In situations where the employee is key but not critical, the seller can get the buyer to agree that the employee's signing of the employment agreement won't be a closing condition – the two parties join together to call the employee's bluff. In situations where the employee is truly critical, the buyer may be willing to split the increased cost of getting the employee's cooperation in order to have a reasonably happy, retainable employee for a stretch of time.

Other problems that are more painful can be solved, but the solution may be a reduction in the purchase price. If a deal hinges on the renewal of a contract with a big customer and the customer leaves for a competitor, there may be no fixing the damage to the business. If the rest of the business has value to the buyer, the buyer may be willing to finish the deal, but with a lower purchase price to reflect the seller's now smaller customer base. Frequently, parties will refer to the new price negotiation as a "re-trade". While a re-trade is never fun, the seller will have to decide whether a lesser deal is better than no deal at all. The seller may decide to take the new price, or perhaps negotiate with the buyer to delay the closing while the seller locates additional new revenue to "refill the bucket". Alternatively, the buyer could agree to set aside some of the purchase price for a year to allow the seller to have time after the closing to accomplish the same thing. If the bucket gets re-filled by the seller's assets, the buyer pays the held back purchase price amount; if not, then the buyer keeps the money.

With a little creativity and trust, most deal killer issues tend to turn into solvable problems.

Conclusion

Reading this chapter, you have now learned how to:

- Properly prepare for a closing and give the parties room to catch problems early enough to fix them through an orchestrated pre-closing.
- Identify gating items
- Resolve "oh my god" deal killer issues that do surface during the pre-closing.

Careful preparation, a cool head and creativity in the face of adversity will get you to the closing nine times out of ten.

Chapter 14: The Closing

What We Will Learn

In this chapter, you will learn about what actually happens at a closing. We will also discuss how busted closings get fixed.

Old School Closings Held In-Person vs. Electronic Closings

Several years ago, nearly every closing would be held in a lawyer's conference room with all of the business leaders present, no matter how big or small a deal was.

The key management team members would literally have to loosen up their wrists, given how many documents they would have to sign. Back in the day, every document would have to be signed multiple times – one set for the buyer, one set for the seller, one set for each law firm and one set for each accountant. Heaven forbid if lenders were involved.

The upside to having clients present was it was pretty easy to ensure that signatures would not be missing. If a deal still had open points or a key consent had not arrived prior to the closing, all of the parties were present and pretty motivated to come up with a solution on the spot.

The downside was having all of the business folks present meant everyone had one last chance to attempt to renegotiate key points. At a minimum, a closing could take hours if one of the CEOs wanted to actually look at every page of each document. Given the downside, I rarely recommend an in-person closing.

The better form these days is for the parties to exchange documents electronically. Normally, the lawyers will finalize the documents and agree that they are ready for signature.

At that point, the lawyers will either send a set of signature pages by .pdf to the buyer and seller to sign and return, or documents will be posted with an electronic signature service like DocuSign or HelloSign. If the electronic signature service is used, the parties will each get an invitation to go to the service's website. The documents will all appear on the site, with markers to show where signatures are required. The party then uses his or her mouse or touchpad to create a signature on the screen and clicks a button to confirm the signature is approved. Once the parties are done signing, the lawyers now have a great record of who signed and when, along with complete documents.

Some lawyers still insist on having each party actually initial every page of every contract, schedule and exhibit. I have been told that these lawyers have seen situations where parties disagreed after a deal about whether a particular schedule was final or not. Personally, I hate making parties sign or initial what can sometimes be literally hundreds of pages. In my mind, the better practice is for the buyer and seller to let the lawyers be orderly and take their time to confirm the final set of documents and then just sign the actual signature pages.

When is the Closing Finished?

If the parties have been organized and actually done the pre-closing described in the previous chapter, the closing itself is pretty simple.

The lawyers confirm with their clients that they are each prepared to close. The executed signature pages had been exchanged during the pre-closing, so now the lawyers just have to let each other know that it is ok to release the executed signature pages out of escrow.

The next step is for the buyer to initiate payment, usually by wire transfer. Once a wire transfer is initiated, the bank sending the wire should receive a "Fed reference number", which is a number that allows the seller to confirm that the wire is really on the way. Wires can take anywhere from half an hour to a few hours to arrive, as they pinball through the banking system. Once the wires have been received at the seller's bank, the closing is usually deemed to be complete.

What Happens if Something Goes Wrong?

Not every closing is pretty.

If the parties did not do a pre-closing, the closing itself could generate quite a bit of excitement.

Things that could go wrong, in no particular order, include:

- The seller is selling its shares in the target company, but nobody remembered to deliver the actual stock certificates for the closing.
- The wire got "lost" in transit.
- The buyer paid by check and the check was: eaten by the copy machine / stuck in a FedEx facility in a storm / made in the name of the wrong party.
- The big customer that promised to send its signed consent did not send it in time for the closing.
- The buyer is paying the seller with shares of the buyer's stock and the buyer's public stock price crashed by 50% the day before the closing.
- The seller's business suffered a "material adverse change" when: a customer worth 25% of the seller's sales cancelled its contract / a key employee died / employees at a seller facility went on strike.

What to do?

The first thing to do is avoid panicking.

Creative parties can always find solutions if a deal is worth completing.

In situations where the buyer has the right to avoid closing because a closing condition wasn't met, the buyer can always waive the closing condition. For example, if the buyer wanted all of the seller's twenty shareholders to sign a non-competition agreement, but one shareholder that owned 1% of the shares won't cooperate, the buyer may just "close over" the requirement and allow the deal to close anyway.

In a situation where a closing condition is not satisfied, but the parties are reasonably sure it will be shortly, the parties may agree to have a side letter allowing the closing condition to be satisfied within a specific period of time in return for the buyer being able to hold back some of the purchase price until the condition is met. For example, imagine part of the business the buyer is purchasing is worth 10% of the purchase price. This portion is located in a country where regulators are notorious for taking their time and need to sign a minor document. If the approval is certain but is just getting delayed, perhaps the buyer will go forward with the larger deal and hold back 10% of the purchase price until the regulatory approval finally arrives.

If the seller's business is materially hurt by an event, the buyer may be willing to close anyway, but will want a price reduction. Buyers frequently will take advantage of the situation and ask for a reduction that may be larger than what the seller believes to be the actual damage. A seller in this situation will have to consider the cost of the reduction versus the cost of not closing the deal and having to continue to run a business that is now damaged by the combination of the negative event and the failed sale.

If the parties decide not to close, Chapter 16 covers what happens in that particular scenario.

Hiding the Ball

Given that the seller could suffer a price reduction if something bad happens to the seller's business, should the seller hide a problem that the seller knows about and just let the buyer come after the seller later for damages or indemnification?

Imagine that your business has a major customer that terminates its contract two days before the closing. You could tell the buyer or not.

The downsides to telling the buyer include having the buyer walk away from the transaction or ask for a major price reduction.

The upsides to disclosing the problem are you have control over how you position the problem and you earn goodwill by disclosing it instead of leaving the buyer to find out about it later. The buyer could very well pursue you for damages or unwind the deal – or both – because you committed fraud. There is also the chance that the buyer finds out about the problem before the closing on its own and gets really angry that you knew about it and didn't say anything. It's also possible and probably likely that if the definitive agreement is well drafted by the buyer, you will have given a covenant to disclose any material adverse events before the closing, so you may get sued under a contractual breach claim.

If you can't tell, I'm a big fan of being honorable and disclosing problems when they come up and working collaboratively to find solutions.

On the flip side, the buyer may discover a problem with your business but not tell you. The buyer then closes the deal and asks for damages or indemnification afterward.

143

If you are in a strong position when you are negotiating the definitive agreement, sometimes you can get a buyer to agree to give a "no sandbagging" representation. The representation requires the buyer to state that the buyer is not aware of any breaches of the seller's representations. Most buyers fight giving this kind of representation like wolverines, on the fear that given enough time and creativity, the seller's lawyers can argue that the buyer knew about a particular bad event based on the giant pile of documents provided during due diligence.

Given that it can be hard to obtain a "no sandbagging" representation, the seller is wise to keep a close eye on the business during the pre-closing phase. As some comfort, I would note that in some states a buyer isn't allowed to seek damages for a problem the buyer knew about and "closed over".

Conclusion

During your review of this chapter, you now have a good idea of what will occur during a closing. You also have an arsenal of possible solutions if your closing gets derailed.

Chapter 15: What Happens After the Closing

What We Will Learn

By reading this chapter, you will learn about:

- The mechanics of what happens immediately after the closing
- Transitional issues

The Victory Lap

Once the closing is officially complete, the seller doesn't get to relax yet.

Next up, the buyer will usually want the seller to do joint meetings with the target company's employees. The buyer wants the employees to see that the seller feels good enough about the buyer to make a joint presentation.

The parties will issue a joint press release as well to announce the deal to the world. On larger deals, the seller might get calls or emails from the media, asking for comments. The key for the seller is to "stay on script" and deliver the message that is helpful to the buyer, but still honest. Close coordination with the buyer on messaging before and after the closing is key.

During the weeks after the deal closes, the buyer may ask the seller for assistance with customers and vendors. The buyer may want the seller to do introductory phone calls, and possibly introductory meetings with larger customers or strategic partners.

Managing the Transition

If you are selling only a part of your business, the buyer may need your remaining business to provide support to the portion that the buyer just purchased.

For example, if the buyer needs time to migrate data from the seller's servers to the buyer's servers, the parties may need to sign a transition services agreement that covers allowing the buyer to access the seller's servers until the data migration is complete. Similarly, if the seller used to provide parts or services to the purchased entity, the buyer may need to continue purchasing these items until the buyer can get a new vendor.

The seller needs to be aware and awake to the fact that the buyer might get used to getting the transitional services from the seller . . . and never actually let the transition end. Consequently, it's very important to make sure that the transitional services agreement is carefully thought out and not done in a rush or on a napkin.

Getting Paid After the Deal

As discussed in prior chapters, many deals will involve payment of the purchase price over time.

If part of the purchase price is held in an escrow or retained by the buyer to cover potential claims for misrepresentations or other indemnification matters, you will want to pay close attention to the dates when funds are supposed to be released to you. If the funds aren't released or the buyer disputes the release, you may have to go through a dispute resolution process usually set forth in the escrow agreement or the definitive agreement. Alternatively, the definitive agreement may require litigation or arbitration to resolve a dispute.

If the business being sold required cash on hand to cover current accounts payable, usually the definitive agreement will have a working capital adjustment. One party will prepare an estimated balance sheet, showing the assets as of the closing date. Usually thirty days or so after the closing, the parties will review the amount of assets actually on hand as of the closing date. If the assets were less than the estimated number, the seller may have to pay the buyer the difference. Similarly, if the assets were greater than the estimated number, the buyer may have to make an additional payment equal to the difference. Usually, the parties have their accounting firms focus on the adjustment and sort out any differences, but the definitive agreement probably has a dispute resolution mechanism specifically geared toward working capital.

Lastly, if the buyer is supposed to pay the seller for future revenue or net income, the seller will need to keep track of future earnout payments.

Managing Yourself after the Closing

Once the deal is over, your world as the seller will have changed. If you are being retained by the buyer, you will find yourself having a boss, possibly for the first time in a very long time. You may also find your employees having to report to folks other than you, and being obligated to respect your employees' new reporting relationships. This can be a very awkward process to go through.

If you are not being retained by the buyer, you may face other anxieties. If you are owed money a year or two after the deal closes because of an escrow or earnout (discussed in previous chapters), you may find yourself worried that the buyer is, or will be, mismanaging the business to your detriment. You may also find yourself having a form of "survivor's guilt" if you just sold a business that you built from scratch or was a family business.

On a more practical level, in the case where you aren't retained by the buyer as an employee, you may still get asked to enter into a consulting arrangement with the buyer for a limited period of time. Here, the buyer wants to be able to absorb any knowledge that the buyer needs to operate the business, have you participate in calls with existing customers and vendors and have you available to sort through any routine issues that come up post-closing. The key factors to consider in negotiating the consulting arrangement are:

- how you will be compensated for your time
- whether any travel will be required
- where the work can be performed (can you provide consulting services by phone or email?)
- how many work hours you are expected to provide
- how long the consulting services will continue

One key to working through the emotional issues is to be self-aware. If things feel weird after you sell your business, take a step back and look at what is causing you to feel a particular emotion. Feelings of loss of authority or being taken advantage of might just be normal after-effects of any sale transaction.

Another key to personal post-deal survival is to have a good support network in place for yourself before you close your deal. Family and friends aren't always the best source of support. Sometimes talking to other business owners, especially ones that have gone through a sale process, can be extraordinarily helpful. You are only as alone as you want to be.

Conclusion

During your review of this chapter, you now have a good idea of what issues are likely to come up after the closing, but mechanically and emotionally.

Chapter 16: When A Deal Needs to be Called Off

What We Will Learn

By reading this chapter, you will learn about:

- how termination rights work;
- what post-termination remedies might be available;
- what needs to happen from a practical standpoint with employees, customers and vendors; and
- how sometimes dead deals come back to life.

Not all deals are meant to be.

While we discussed solutions to potential deal-breakers in Chapter 13, if your business loses a key customer before the closing and the price reduction demanded by the buyer is too steep, you may decide not closing is your best option. Your deal may also get derailed by factors outside your control like a lawsuit by the government to stop your deal if the combination of your business with the buyer's business is deemed by the government to be likely to hurt competition on the marketplace.

Termination Rights

Virtually every purchase agreement will contain a section covering termination rights. Normally, the section will offer three routes to bring the deal to an end:

- The parties both agree in writing to walk away.
- One party walks away because the other party materially breached the terms of the deal.
- The deal takes so long that the closing has not occurred by a specific date, called a "drop dead

149

date" and one of the parties elects to terminate the deal for failure to close by the drop dead date.

In a deal where the government sues to prevent the deal, the parties may choose the first option and just agree in writing to terminate the deal. Neither side failed to meet its obligations, the deal just couldn't close because of the suit.

If one party decides the other party materially breached the terms of the purchase agreement (i.e., the seller gave all of its employees a 20% pay increase when the seller had promised in the document not to do anything "outside the ordinary course of its business"), normally the purchase agreement will have language requiring the terminating party to give the "breaching" party a period of time to fix the breach before the termination becomes final.

If neither party breached the agreement but one party wants to still drag things out past a reasonable "drop dead date", it's common for each party to be able to walk away from the deal. However, the section permitting termination after a drop dead date will also usually only allow this kind of termination by a party that didn't intentionally cause the deal to drag out by making sure that one of the key closing conditions that the terminating party was supposed to make happen failed to actually occur.

Remedies and Liabilities

If a deal dies because of something like the previously mentioned government lawsuit, usually the parties walk away without looking to sue each other.

In situations where one party has a lot of leverage, one side may have requested a "breakup fee" and will actually get paid by the other party if the deal terminates. Breakup fees are not common, but will appear in deals where one party has enough leverage to request one, or has had bad experiences on other deals that cause the request to get made.

The request for a breakup fee usually comes during the negotiation of the letter of intent, since its inclusion in the purchase agreement without prior discussion can be incendiary.

If the buyer asks for a breakup fee, the buyer's logic in making the request runs along the lines of the buyer's reluctance to invest legal fees, accounting fees, investment banker fees, travel expenses and management time performing due diligence on the target company and having lawyers negotiate and draft documents for a deal that goes nowhere. Sometimes in keeping with this argument, the breakup fee will be specifically tied to a scenario where the seller's behavior caused the deal to fail, but the buyer may ask for the breakup fee to be paid on any termination.

If the seller has the leverage, the seller may ask for a non-refundable "good faith" deposit from the buyer to confirm the buyer is serious before the seller spends money on legal fees, accounting fees, etc. In this scenario, the termination section would make the seller's right to keep the deposit clear.

In more typical deals, the termination section won't include a breakup fee but will have language reserving each party's rights to pursue claims for damages caused by the other party's material breaches of the purchase agreement after termination.

If one party is particularly angry, the party could go to court asking for "specific performance." Here, the party is asking the court to force the other party to perform their obligations under the purchase agreement – effectively requiring a closing. Different courts in different states have a wide variety of reactions to a demand for specific performance, largely depending on the behavior of the parties and the law in the state where the demand is made. Getting specific performance can be a hard, expensive road.

151

The Morning After – What Happens to the Target Business on a Failed Deal

If your deal doesn't close, you will have a lot of work to do. This section tries to anticipate what you will need to address.

If you are in the later stages of a deal when termination comes, your employees may have been aware of the pending deal. It's best to make some kind of announcement, but to wait until the termination is actually effective – otherwise if the "deal breaker" on Monday gets resolved by a change of heart by the buyer on Tuesday, you may find that you inadvertently breached a promise in the purchase agreement that you wouldn't damage relationships with the employees or discourage them from wanting to join the buyer after the deal.

When you address your work force, you want to address why the deal terminated in simple terms. Regardless of how angry you may be if you felt the buyer did something wrong, you probably want to avoid using a speech to employees to blast the buyer's behavior for the same reason discussed in the prior paragraph – the deal could come back.

Statements that the parties were just too far apart on the final price but agreed to potentially reconsider a deal in the future may soften the blow. If the business lost a major customer two days before the closing, the employees probably know about the loss and can understand that caused the parties to "pause" while the business refills its customer roster.

The key thing is to think like an employee when addressing the work force. They want to know if their jobs are safe. They want to know that you have faith in the business and in them.

The same thing is true with your customer base. If the customers were contacted with requests for contract consents or as part of the buyer's diligence, you will want to pro-actively reach out to them quickly after the deal is formally terminated. They will also want comfort that the business is healthy and their needs will continue to be met.

It might be easy to overlook vendors, but you will want to do the same drill for vendors. If you don't reach out to vendors, they may worry and start asking for shorter payment terms or security deposits. Better to head off these consequences with friendly phone calls to give them assurance.

On a final note, while you may be physically and emotionally spent after a deal terminates, you may want to consider the optics of going on a long vacation immediately after the termination. All of your constituencies need the speeches and phone calls, but they will judge whether your words were true by your actions, so try not to look beaten, whether you are or not.

When a Dead Deal Comes Back to Life

As a lawyer, I have represented a number of buyers that called off deals. The deals have died because of a regulatory change, a discovery in diligence that the anticipated revenue just wasn't there or that a key customer was unwilling to give their consent to the sale to my client.

On more occasions than I can count on both hands, I have seen "dead" deals come back to life months, sometimes years later. At the time of this writing, I am working on a deal that died thirteen months ago but came roaring back.

Deals come back to life for a variety of reasons.

On the buyer's side of the table, sometimes the buyer decides that their growth requires buying the seller's business because of problems the buyer's operations are having in the seller's market segment or geographic location. The buyer might be preparing to actually sell itself and needs to show acquirors that its own company has a strong presence that it can get only by gobbling up the seller. In these situations, the buyer may be willing to drop its request for a purchase price reduction over a lost customer or look past a failure to get a key customer consent.

On the seller's side, you may find that the price reduction that you were offered when you lost a key customer three months ago looks much better months later. You may also find that management changed at the difficult customer's company and now you can get the customer consent that killed the first version of your deal.

Scenarios like the ones above are why I try to encourage sellers to never burn bridges with buyers. While losing a deal can feel a lot like someone rejecting your child, keeping emotions under control can generate a payday tomorrow.

Conclusion

By reading this chapter, you have now learned:

- How a deal can be terminated;
- What the consequence of termination might look like;
- Strategies for handling the aftermath of a terminated deal at your company; and
- How deals might get revived.

Appendix A – Examples of Tax Impact for Different Sale Structures

The tax impact on a sale can be dramatically different depending on the tax status of the target company and the way the sale transaction is treated for tax purposes.

As in all things tax-related, make sure to consult a tax professional. The examples here are for illustrative purposes only and are not meant to be advice. They do not address potential planning opportunities connected to C corporation taxation or thorny issues like "hot assets" which can trigger ordinary income tax rates rather than long-term capital gain or dividend tax rates.

Example 1: Buyer buys shares of stock from two shareholders of a corporation.

Buyer pays $10MM for the shares of Widget Corp. from two shareholders. The shareholders each hold shares equal to 50% of Widget's stock. This means each shareholder gets $5MM.

Shareholder 1 paid $250,000 for her stock. She may have paid for it at the formation of the company, or more likely paid in extra capital over time, but either way, her "basis" in her shares is $250,000.

When Shareholder 1 received $5MM from the buyer, $250,000 of the payment is treated as a return of capital, and is tax-free. The remaining $4.75MM is profit on the sale of Shareholder 1's shares.

Assuming Shareholder 1 held her shares for more than one year, the profit is classified as "long-term capital gain". The $4.75MM will be taxed at the federal level and again at the state level. Applying the long-term capital gain rate at each level, in a state like California the combined tax bill will equal 30-33% of the profit, or approximately $1.5MM.

Shareholder 1 would get $3.25MM after taxes.

Example 2: Buyer buys the assets of a C corporation.

Buyer pays $10MM for the assets of Widget Corp.

Widget Corp. has to pay taxes on the asset sale at the corporation's ordinary income tax rates – unlike for individuals, there is no preferential C corporation rate for long-term capital gain rates - at both the federal and state level. In a state like California, the combined rate would be equal to 43%, or $4.3MM.

The remaining $5.7MM would be left for Widget Corp. to distribute to its shareholders. Since Widget Corp. is a C corporation, any distributions get taxed again, as long-term capital gain.

Assume the shareholders each had $250,000 of paid-in capital contributions for their shares. This lowers the total taxable amount of the $5.7MM by $500K.

The distribution to the shareholders would be taxed at the long-term capital gains rate at the federal level. State level taxation of capital gain varies. California, for instance, taxes all income with the same rate regardless of the nature of the income. So, in our example, a California resident would have a combined rate of 30-36%, or an approximate $1.6 – 1.9MM tax bite out of $5.2MM taxable profit.

The end result: the shareholders ultimately get about $4MM out of $10MM after taxes.

Note: An important consideration when dealing with C corporations is something called "Qualified Small Business Stock" (QSBS). Special provisions in the tax code allow for potentially significant tax breaks if you qualify. Additionally, you may have the option of deferring taxes on capital gains by reinvesting sales proceeds into another QSBS corporation. Again, consult your tax advisor.

Example 3: Buyer buys the assets of an S corporation

Buyer pays $10MM for the assets of Widget Corp.

Widget Corp. is treated as a "pass-through entity" for tax purposes, so there is no tax on the $10MM paid to the corporation. The entire $10MM is available for distribution by Widget Corp. to its shareholders.

Assume the shareholders had $250,000 of paid-in capital contributions for their shares. This lowers the taxable amount of the $10MM by $500K.

The $9.5MM taxable portion of the distribution is taxed at long term capital gain rates at the federal and state level, at a combined rate of 30-33%, for a tax bite around $3.1MM.

The end result: the shareholders ultimately get a combined $6.9MM out of $10MM after taxes.

Note: The buyer may want to make a 338(h)(10) election, discussed in Chapter 9. The buyer wants to get the value of a "step up" or increase in the basis of the assets of Widget Corp., even though the buyer bought the stock of Widget Corp. The buyer can get this "step up" because Widget Corp. was an S corporation.

The step up may create significant tax benefits for the buyer, since the buyer can write off the depreciation of the assets from its taxes. However, the election will cause the sellers to have an increase in their taxes. Usually, the buyer will pay a higher purchase price to get the seller's cooperation because the depreciation benefits typically far outweigh the cost of "grossing up" the sales price to eliminate the tax hit for the seller.

Acknowledgements

I have a number of people I would like to thank for their help in inspiring and building this book and the new edition.

I was very lucky to have great corporate finance lawyers as models early in my career. Linda Williams at Pillsbury Winthrop Shaw Pittman taught me a great deal about professionalism during my first few years of large law firm practice. Bruce Mann, a true legend and terrific mentor, trusted me with my first deal to run at Morrison & Foerster and gave me the confidence to be my own guy. Gavin Grover, also with Morrison & Foerster, taught me about the ins and outs of the behind-the-scenes world of practicing law and guided me through significant challenges.

Mike Bowen was my original mentor when I was a wide-eyed undergrad student at the University of Notre Dame. He gave me the tools to be an independent thinker and strategist, instead of just becoming another tactician.

A number of friends were gracious enough to read and comment on early versions of the chapters contained in the first edition of this book, including Bill Staley, Louis Hamel, Addison McCaleb and Wes Burger. I'm particularly thankful for the tax examples that Louis Hamel contributed. They have my gratitude for wading through the bits and pieces that were ultimately weeded out.

Angela Bandich did a great job of streamlining this tome and keeping her boss sane. It has been fun watching her grow as a bright, young lawyer.

I would also like to thank my clients, current and past. You were the inspiration for this book. The journey of being a deal lawyer is fast and fluid -- you make it fun.

41471156R00091

Made in the USA
San Bernardino, CA
13 November 2016